R2003675192 06/16

✳ *Influential Latinos* ✳

ISABEL ALLENDE

Award-Winning Author

Jeanne Nagle and Mary Main

Enslow Publishing
101 W. 23rd Street
Suite 240
New York, NY 10011
USA

enslow.com

Published in 2016 by Enslow Publishing, LLC
101 W. 23rd Street, Suite 240, New York, NY 10011

Library of Congress Cataloging-in-Publication Data
Nagle, Jeanne.
Isabel Allende : award-winning author / Jeanne Nagle and Mary Main.
    pages cm. — (Influential Latinos)
Includes bibliographical references and index.
Summary: "Describes the life and accomplishments of Latina writer Isabel Allende"— Provided by publisher.
ISBN 978-0-7660-7250-3
1. Allende, Isabel—Juvenile literature. 2. Authors, Chilean—20th century—Biography—Juvenile literature. I. Main, Mary. II. Title.
PQ8098.1.L54Z79 2016
863'.64—dc23
[B]
                    2015029845

Printed in the United States of America

To Our Readers: We have done our best to make sure all website addresses in this book were active and appropriate when we went to press. However, the author and the publisher have no control over and assume no liability for the material available on those websites or on any websites they may link to. Any comments or suggestions can be sent by e-mail to customerservice@enslow.com.

Portions of this book originally appeared in *Isalbel Allende Award-Winning Latin American Author* by Mary Main

Photo Credits: Cover, p. 1 Alfonso Jimenez Valero/Getty Images Entertainment/Getty Images; p. 4 Horst Tappe/Archive Photos/Getty Images; p. 7 Michael Mauny/The LIFE Images Collection/Getty Images; p. 11 Jan E Carlsson/AFP/Getty Images; p.15 © iStockphoto.com/traveler1116; p.18 MyLoupe/UIG Via Getty Images; p. 21 London Stereoscopic Company/Stringer/Hulton Archive/Getty Images; p. 23 Marcelo Hernandez/Latin Content/Getty Images; p.27 Ulrich Baumgarten/Getty Images; pp. 30, 51 Roger Viollet/Getty Images; pp. 33, 47 ullstein bild/Getty Images; p. 37 Diamond Images/Getty Images; pp. 41, 58 Felipe Amilibia/AFP/Getty Images; p. 43 David Fenton/Archive Photos/Getty Images; p. 52 Keystone/Hulton Archive/Getty Images; p. 56 Paul Conklin/Archive Photos/Getty Images; p. 61 AP Photo/Marty Lederhandler; p. 63 Steve Eason/Hulton Archive/Getty Images; p. 64 Ulf Andersen/Hulton Archive/Getty Images; p. 67 Keystone-France/Gamma-Keystone/Getty Images; p.69 Acey Harper/The LIFE Images Collection/Getty Images; p. 71 Cindy Karp/The LIFE Images Collection/Getty Images; p. 74 AP Photo/Eric Risberg; p. 79 Mondadori/Portfolio/Getty Images; p. 81© United Archives GmbH / Alamy; pp. 83, 92 The Boston Globe via Getty Images; p. 87 ©AP Images; p. 83 Victor Rojas/AFP/Getty Images; p. 94 Koen can Weel/AFP/Getty Images; p. 98 The Print Collector/Print Collector/Hulton Archive/Getty Images; p. 104 CLAUS FISKER/AFP/Getty Images; p. 106 MANDEL NGAN/AFP/Getty Images.

Contents

Although she had written stories all her life, it wasn't until Isabel Allende was nearly forty that she wrote her first novel. The success of *The House of the Spirits* would change the former journalist's life.

Chapter 1

A Spiritual Undertaking

In January 1981, Isabel Allende was living a different life than any she might have envisioned for herself. A seasoned print and television journalist from Santiago, Chile, Allende found herself working long hours as a school administrator in Caracas, Venezuela instead. She, her husband, and two children were squeezed into a small apartment. Her mother and step-father lived in another apartment one floor above. The neighborhood was filled with noisy traffic and the sounds of people yelling and fighting. Caracas did not suit Allende. She longed for "the peace of a forest, the silence of a mountain, the whisper of the sea" she cherished in her homeland.[1]

Allende and her family had left Chile five years earlier to escape the military dictatorship that had overthrown Chile's government. Allende's father was the cousin of the country's former president, Salvador Allende, who had been killed in the fight for control. She was afraid that government forces would target members of Salvador's family. Like it or not, at least life in Caracas was relatively safe for the family.

Allende's homesickness got even worse when she received word that her one-hundred-year-old grandfather was gravely ill. She wanted to see her Tata (Grandpa) one last time, but knew she could not return home.

Then she remembered something her grandfather had told her. He said that people only truly die when they are forgotten.[2] In an attempt to assure Tata that he had not been forgotten by her, Allende decided to write her grandfather a letter filled with family stories. She set up her portable typewriter and wrote late into the night. As words flowed through her fingers, her homesickness was transformed into energy and enthusiasm.

Reality Spiced With Magic

Allende began her letter with the story of her grandfather's first love, a beautiful and mysterious great-aunt who had died from poisoning. Then she added even more intrigue to the family history. To represent her great-aunt, she created a woman with white skin, green hair, and gold eyes who looked like a mermaid. She named her Rosa. In Rosa the Beautiful's character, family truths mingled with traits from Allende's imagination.[3]

Allende spiced up her story with wacky events. In one scene, Uncle Marcos builds a giant bird and flies off over a mountain range. A week after the family mourns at his funeral, he comes walking out of the mountains, happy and healthy. In another scene, the character Clara

When Chilean president Salvador Allende was overthrown in a military coup, Chile became a dangerous place for the Allendes.

searches for her mother's head, which had been severed from the older woman's body in a car crash. Clara finds the head by the side of the road, looking like a "lonely melon."[4] She hides it in a leather hatbox in the basement. Twenty years later, the family finds it and sets it next to Clara in her coffin.

Allende drew on actual events in her own life to create many of her scenes. Two events inspired the severed head incident. The first is that Allende had a friend whose parents were killed in a car crash, and the mother was decapitated in the accident. The sons had to retrieve the head from under some bushes. The other incident was from Allende's childhood. After she found a skull in the basement of her grandfather's house, she started using it in some of her games.

Combining real events with imaginative ways of looking at the world is a type of writing known as "magical realism."[5] Strange and supernatural events are incorporated into Allende's books as though they actually happened.[6] To Allende, magic realism is "something mysterious or difficult to explain that happens in real life—ESP, premonitions, prophetic dreams, incredible coincidences."[7]

Birth of a Novel

Her letter was turning into something Allende had not expected. It was turning into a novel. Allende had spent twenty years as a journalist and playwright in Chile. She could not imagine herself as a novelist. In fact, the idea made her feel a bit arrogant, but she was having too much fun to stop.

Every day, Allende tied a ribbon around her manuscript and took it to work in a canvas satchel, keeping it close to her. At night, she sat at her typewriter and let the story pour out onto paper. Even the news that Tata had died did not dampen her enthusiasm for writing. Allende felt the spirits of her grandparents in the room, guiding her words. She believed that Memé (Grandma) and Tata were helping her create the exciting saga of the del Valle and Trueba families.

One day, Allende realized that she had written five hundred pages. It was time to end her novel, but how? She was stumped for ideas until Tata came to her in a

From Letters to a Novel

For centuries writers have been telling stories through letter writing. Gathering together several letters to make a story, as Allende did with her letters to her grandfather, creates what is known as an epistolary novel. The term comes from the word "epistle," which is the Greek word for "letter" or "message." While letters are the most common form of epistolary text, journal or diary entries, e-mail messages, and even texts may also be used. Authors can create epistolary novels using either real letters or messages written specifically for a character or characters in a story. Epistolary novels were quite popular in the 1700s. More recent epistolary novels include *The Princess Diaries* by Meg Cabot and Stephen Chbosky's *The Perks of Being a Wallflower.*

dream to give her the answer. In the dream, Allende approached the bed where her grandfather slept. When she picked up the sheet, she saw that he was dead. This dream gave her the idea of having the granddaughter in the book sit beside the body of her grandfather as she tells the story. Allende woke from the dream at three o'clock in the morning. She hurried to the kitchen and typed a ten-page epilogue without stopping.

Dreams and Imagination in Print

Allende's mother helped choose the title for her daughter's novel—*The House of the Spirits*. She also persuaded Allende to try to publish the book. They sent letters to publishers, but no one wrote back. Finally, Allende heard about a literary agent in Barcelona, Spain, named Carmen Balcells. A literary agent advises authors and helps sell their books to publishing houses. Allende mailed the manuscript to Balcells, who agreed to be Allende's agent. Six months later, *The House of the Spirits* was published in Spain, with an image of green-haired Rosa the Beautiful on the cover.

In Madrid, Spain's capital, Balcells threw a lavish party for Allende. All the celebrities in Spanish literary circles were there. Allende could not believe she deserved such recognition. How would she talk to all these brilliant people? "I was so frightened I spent a good part of the evening hiding in the bathroom," she said later.[8]

In 1985, *The House of the Spirits* was translated into English and published in the United States by the respected publishing house Alfred A. Knopf. The novel

Allende became known for writing in the magical realism style. This genre allows for the presence of magic in the natural world.

became an international best seller. Allende had taken the literary world by storm. In the midst of sadness and separation from her grandfather and her beloved homeland of Chile, Isabel Allende penned one of the most popular family sagas of the twentieth century and was propelled to international success.[9]

Chapter 2

A Bumpy Childhood

Isabel Allende has said that writing *The House of the Spirits* was like opening a floodgate and letting out a torrent. "I never recovered from the tremendous impact of that torrent," she has said. "It changed my life."[1]

That was the start of her life as a novelist. Isabel experienced a flood of emotions throughout the early years of her actual life as well. Events that greatly influenced her beliefs and actions included abandonment by her father, her parents' divorce, moving into the strict household of her maternal grandparents, the death of her grandmother, and the remarriage of her mother.

Early Years

Isabel Allende was born on August 2, 1942, in Lima, Peru. Although her parents were from Chile, they were living in Peru. Her father, Tomás Allende, was Secretary of the Chilean Embassy. Her mother, Francisca Llona Barros Allende, was a homemaker. Isabel and her two younger brothers, Francisco (called Pancho) and Juan, were all born in Peru.

World War II was raging across Europe and the Pacific at the time of Isabel's birth. American soldiers were fighting with the Allied Forces of Great Britain and the Soviet Union against Japan and Germany. Although much of the world was unstable then, World War II did not reach Latin America, where Isabel's family lived.

In 1945, when Isabel was three years old, her parents separated. The Chilean consul in Peru, a man named Ramón Huidobro, helped Francisca book passage on a boat leaving Peru. Francisca gathered her three children, their nanny Margara, and their dog Pelvina López-Pun, and sailed home to Chile. Isabel never spoke to her father, Tomás Allende, again. All photographs of him were burned, and his name was never mentioned.[2] When Isabel asked questions about him, she was told only that he was a very intelligent gentleman.[3]

Chile is a Catholic country with strict religious beliefs, and at that time divorce was forbidden. Isabel's mother had her marriage annulled by the Catholic Church, which declared that a valid marriage had never existed. Many people criticized Francisca for ending her unhappy marriage, but her family supported her decision. Her relatives had never approved of the marriage between Francisca and Tomás, because he was fifteen years older than she and did not embrace the family's religious beliefs.[4]

The change from protected wife to single mother was not easy for Isabel's mother. Francisca Allende, known as "Panchita," had been raised in an affluent home and admired as the most beautiful girl in her family. Growing

Isabel Allende was born in Lima, Peru, but she moved to Chile, the home of her mother's family, at the age of three.

up, she spent her time going to school, reading romantic novels, and doing charitable works. She had lived a privileged life. After the separation from her husband, Panchita had come home to her family in Chile.

Life With Memé and Tata

At home in Santiago, three-year-old Isabel, her mother, and her brothers moved into her grandparents' colonial-style home on Suecia Street. Heavy, dark furniture, considered the finest of its time, decorated the house. Dark red upholstery covered the sofas and chairs that filled the drafty rooms. A grand piano and a crystal chandelier dominated the living room. When the huge black grandfather clock struck the hour, it sounded like funeral bells to Isabel.[5] In spite of its gloomy furnishings, the house was lively, filled with exotic animals, visitors, and music.

Isabel's grandfather Agustín Llona Cuevas was a successful businessman. He raised sheep in the southern portion of the country, in Patagonia, and then exported the wool to England. Tata provided everything his family needed. A staff of servants cared for the family, including Isabel's two uncles, who lived with them. Isabel's grandfather was extremely religious and conservative. He believed that men were superior to women and children, who must be guided and protected. This belief is known as patriarchy. As a self-made man and the patriarch of the family, Tata had many strong opinions. He taught Isabel that life is hard and that the highest goal is success.[6]

Facts About Chile

Chile resembles a long, thin, winding ribbon along the southwest coast of South America. The country stretches 2,700 miles from top to bottom, equal to the distance from San Francisco to New York, and is no wider than 150 miles. It is a land of lush valleys, soaring mountains, and wild seas. Earthquakes, volcanic eruptions, and floods occur regularly. The climate is a study in contrasts, hot in the northern deserts and often cold and rainy in the south. There are also many mild days, much like the weather in California.

Isabel's grandmother Isabel Barros Moreira, who was known as Memé, was interested and active in paranormal activity. Paranormal refers to things that cannot be easily explained using science, and may be influenced by supernatural spirits. "My grandmother was always experimenting with the paranormal," Allende has said. "She would have these séances, experiment with telepathy, trying to move objects without touching them, and guess what was inside a box that was closed."[7]

It also was said that Memé could send items such as the sugar bowl skittering across the table using only her mind. A small silver bell, its handle in the image of a prince, sat at Memé's place at the dinner table. Once, after a dinner party, Isabel claimed that she and the guests had watched, awestruck, as the bell slid across the tablecloth, made a wide turn, and then returned to Memé's place at the foot of the table.[8]

The world with its meanness, violence, and vulgarity was often too much for Memé. At those times, Isabel's grandmother retreated from life to roam the halls, lost in her own dreamy silence. Memé refused to dial a telephone and said she used mental telepathy to exchange recipes with her friends the Mora sisters, who lived on the other side of the city. She spent the majority of her time visiting the slums to help people, sewing, and collecting money for the poor.

When Memé died from leukemia, the house sank into mourning. Tata wore all black clothing and insisted that everyone else in the house do the same. He had the furniture painted black and gave the order that there would be no parties, music, flowers, or desserts. He eliminated anything that might bring cheer to the household and disturb his grief for his beloved wife. Silence spread through the house, and it became a dark, ugly, cold place for Isabel. She imagined that spirits haunted the corridors and that Satan lived inside the mirrors.

A Girl and Her Stories

At that time, there was no television in Chile, and Tata did not allow the radio to be turned on very often. To ease her unhappiness, Isabel escaped into stories. Books overflowed the shelves and desk of her Uncle Pablo's room, providing an instant library for the curious young

Isabel lived comfortably in Chile, thanks in part to her grandfather's lucrative sheep farm in Patagonia.

girl. Since her grandfather had a strict rule of lights out at nine o'clock, Uncle Pablo gave her a flashlight. She hid books under the covers to read at night. Adventure stories and detective novels were her favorites. She also devoured Spanish translations of sophisticated novels such as *Anna Karenina* and *Les Miserables*. Her uncle rewarded her with a doll when she completed *War and Peace*. As she read, she longed for romantic and violent things to happen in the stories.[9]

The cellar of the big house was a wonderful place to escape. There Isabel played make-believe games, reading by candlelight, dreaming of magic castles, and dressing up like a ghost. Her active imagination led her to use an entire series of discarded books to build forts. She would then fall asleep in her imaginary kingdom.

In the cellar Isabel also found a trunk filled with books abandoned by her father. The trunk was the only proof Isabel had ever seen that her father existed. Novels written by Jules Verne, Emilio Salgari, Charles Dickens, and other authors filled the trunk. Captivated by the mystery surrounding her father, Isabel read the books voraciously. Yet her questions about her father remained unanswered.

Dark and Light Moments

Isabel's mother, Panchita, found a full time job at a local bank but did not earn enough money to support her children without help from Uncle Pablo and Tata. Panchita supplemented her income by making and selling beautiful hats. All the stress of trying to make ends meet gave her terrible headaches that sent her to bed for two or three days at a time. Isabel was terrified her mother would die and she would be sent to live with her father. Since it was forbidden to speak about her father, she could not tell anyone about her fears.[10]

Margara, the children's nanny, took control. If the children disobeyed her orders, she hit them with a leather strap. Isabel later described Margara as a tyrant who tried to separate the children from their mother. She would bathe, feed, and put the children to bed before Panchita came home from work. If Isabel and her brothers were still awake when their mother arrived, Magara ordered them not to disturb her.

Often, Isabel and her brothers ignored Magara and tiptoed into their mother's room at night. There, the three children listened with rapt attention as Panchita told them stories about their ancestors. In Panchita's imaginary world, everyone was happy. These family times inspired a love of storytelling in Isabel.[11] She loved to torture her brothers with horrifying tales that scared them so much they could not sleep.

Recognizing her daughter's gift for creativity, Panchita allowed Isabel to paint whatever she wanted on the walls of her room. Isabel painted friends, animals, and landscapes.

On an occasional Sunday, the family would trek to the top of San Cristóbal, a hill in the center of the city. Salvador Allende, a cousin of Isabel's father, and his wife, Hortensia, sometimes joined them with their three daughters and their dogs. Salvador Allende was a doctor and a well-known socialist politician in Chile. Isabel called him "Uncle Salvador." On those Sunday afternoons, the family picnicked on chicken and hard-boiled eggs and played games.

Still, even these pleasant times were tinged with the dark side. Roars of lions from the city zoo echoed

Isabel was captivated by the works of British novelist Charles Dickens, whose works were among the books left behind by Isabel's father.

through the hillside as the big cats were fed live animals. Isabel and her cousins imagined that dinner for the lions came from the animal shelter, and they cringed in horror at the roars.[12]

A Rough Trip

Isabel was still very young when Tata took her to visit Patagonia in the south to watch sheep being sheared of their wool. It was a difficult journey, and Isabel was violently carsick. Once they arrived at their destination, mules carried them over mountain passes into the wilderness. Isabel was thrown to the ground twice. But she was enchanted by the huge ferns and tree trunks and snow-covered volcanoes in the high mountain passes. Her love for her homeland of Chile grew even stronger on this trip.

The sheep shearing shocked Isabel with its cruelty. The workers were paid by the animal. The faster they sliced the wool off the sheep, the more money they earned. Sometimes strips of the animal's skin came off along with the wool. The bleeding animal was then stitched up and returned to the herd in the hopes it would survive.

In the evenings, the herdsmen would kill a lamb and roast it on a spit. Isabel and Tata sat with the men. They ate the roasted meat and washed it down with *mate*, a green, bitter tea served in a gourd. The herdsmen passed around the gourd and everyone sipped from the same metal straw. By the time the gourd came to Isabel, the straw was slippery with spit and chewing tobacco. But she had to take her turn. To refuse would have been bad manners and an insult to the herders.

The Prince Becomes Real

Isabel's family spent summers at the shore, where they owned a huge, damp house. At that time, the car trip took a whole day. The entire family, including the parrot and the dog, Pelvina López-Pun, made the trip in Tata's black English touring car. Isabel and the others suffered terrible carsickness on those rides. But once at the shore, Isabel forgot about her nausea. La Playa Grande was

Among Isabel Allende's favorite childhood memories are Sunday visits to San Cristobal, Santiago's second-highest peak.

beautiful. Children played on the beach all morning with nannies and mothers. Margara tied the children to her with ropes so they could safely splash in the water while she knit sweaters and Isabel's mother sunbathed. At two o'clock, they all went home for lunch and a siesta.

At the end of the day, Panchita would take Isabel's hand and lead her to a place where they could watch the sunset. There, one day, she told Isabel that she was in love with a man named Ramón Huidobro. He was a diplomat who worked in the embassy in Peru—the man who had helped the family return to Chile after Panchita left Isabel's father. Isabel imagined Huidobro as an enchanted prince living in a far-off land in a fairy tale. Fear that her mother would marry Ramón and abandon her and her brothers gripped Isabel.[13] Because of this fear, she was glad the prince lived far, far away.[14]

Back in Santiago, Isabel was surprised one day when Ramón Huidobro came to visit. Convinced that he was imaginary, she could hardly believe he was a real person and was in love with her mother. Far from the handsome prince of her fantasies, Isabel thought the real Ramón was the ugliest man she had ever seen. The man she would come to call Tío Ramón (Uncle Ramón) would change her life in many ways. In 1952, when Isabel was ten years old, her mother and Tío Ramón decided to marry. Tío Ramón was assigned as a diplomat to the country of Bolivia. Panchita and her three children would go with him to the city of La Paz.

Chapter 3

STORIES ON THE ROAD

O
n the night before Isabel was to leave for Bolivia with her mother, new stepfather and siblings, she crept downstairs while everyone else slept to speak with the spirit of her grandmother. In her very active imagination, Isabel believed that Memé could be reached somewhere within the folds of the drawing room drapes. As Allende would later tell the story, the spirit of Memé suggested she take a memento from her and Tata's house. Specifically, the spirit told Isabel to find and keep a silver mirror that was tucked away in Tata's bedroom. By looking in this mirror, Isabel would feel as if her grandmother was right there with her wherever she went.

Careful not to wake Tata, Isabel tiptoed into the bedroom, searching the bureau drawers for the special mirror. She managed to rummage around, grab the mirror, and get back out of the bedroom without waking her grandfather. Safely back in her own bed, Isabel dared to look into the mirror, to see if Memé would actually appear. Relying mainly on her imagination, she thought she saw her grandmother in the mirror's glassy surface, telling her good-night.[1] Perhaps the move to Bolivia would not be as scary or lonesome as she might have thought.

Journaling Saves the Day

Early the next morning, Isabel added the word *adíos* (good-bye) to the mural on her bedroom wall. The family spent the day packing suitcases and tying them on top of the cars they would drive to the port. They would take a ship, then a train high into the Andes Mountains. Isabel was leaving her home, her country, and her beloved grandfather to travel to an unknown place. Tata stood in the doorway, dressed all in black, waving goodbye. She felt as if her childhood ended at that moment.[2]

On the journey, Panchita gave Isabel a notebook and suggested she write about her travels. Isabel wrote about all the sights, sounds, and smells she experienced on the way to Bolivia. Writing in the notebook helped Isabel understand her feelings and gave her a sense of what was real. From that time on, Isabel has written in her notebook nearly every day. She says it helps her "sort out the confusion of life."[3]

La Paz was a beautiful city high in the Andes Mountains. The family moved into a compound of three houses that shared a common garden. In the quiet of the garden, Isabel found hiding places for her notebook and some hideouts where she could read and write in solitude.

Forging Bonds in a New Land

One day at Isabel's new school, the teacher said that soldiers from Chile had committed brutal acts against the people of other countries during wartime. Isabel had always believed that her country was the best in the world. She was sure that her country would never do bad things. When she spoke up, the teacher ordered her to stand in the hallway.[4] Isabel stood there, fighting back tears. After a few minutes, she noticed she was not the only one being punished. A dark-haired boy with very large ears stood in the opposite corner, his face to the wall.

When she was ten, Isabel moved with her family to La Paz, Bolivia, where her new stepfather was assigned as a diplomat.

Isabel developed a crush on the boy and began writing stories about him in her notebooks. He ignored Isabel, acting as if she did not exist. The other kids in school knew she liked the boy with the big ears and made fun of her. Isabel's first crush ended in unexpected chaos. One day she and the boy ended up in a big fight on the playground. Isabel bit the boy's ear. Far from being upset about it, Isabel enjoyed the tussle.[5]

Her crush was not the only person of the opposite sex with whom Isabel had to work out a relationship while in La Paz. She had mixed feelings about Tío Ramón, but would eventually come to think of him as her true father.[6] He believed in training children to be strong and independent. He taught Isabel and her brothers that they should have goals and move steadily toward those goals.[7]

Tío Ramón gave Isabel the complete works of William Shakespeare as a gift. She read Shakespeare's plays over and over, just as other kids read comic books. The stories of murderous kings and passionate lovers fired up her imagination and prepared her for the writer she would one day become. "I would draw the characters on cardboard, cut them out, paste a stick behind them and act out the plays," she said later.[8]

New Surroundings, New Culture

In 1955, when Isabel was twelve years old, Tío Ramón was given another diplomatic position, this time in Beirut, Lebanon. Isabel and her family had to move once again. Tío Ramón flew to Paris en route to his new post in Beirut. Isabel and her brothers traveled back home to Chile with their mother, then to Genoa and Rome, Italy. From Rome, they went to Beirut to rejoin Tío Ramón. The journey took two months.

In Beirut, the family lived in a big apartment. Isabel would often sit at the window of the apartment, peering at the activities in the streets below. There she saw automobiles and camels and fancy Cadillacs driven by rich sheikhs. There were Muslim women dressed all in black, totally covered except for a peephole for their eyes. Enchanted by the music, sounds, and smells of the city, she felt as if she were locked away in a prison.[9]

Beirut was a busy and fascinating place. At that time, it was considered the Paris of the Middle East, the center of culture and business. Several times a day, Isabel heard the high, wailing sounds of the religious men calling the faithful to prayer along with bells chiming atop Christian churches. Isabel would often shop with her mother in the souks—narrow alleyways lined with shops selling everything from food to clothing to antiques. Every aroma imaginable wafted from the alleys. Delicious smells of exotic foods and perfumes mingled with the stink of garbage and sewage floating in open drains.

Isabel's mother had a difficult time adjusting to the culture and hot weather in Lebanon. She also wished her family were rich like the other diplomats' families. Still, Panchita made the best of her circumstances, sewing herself a beautiful dress to wear to diplomatic events. She decorated the apartment with paintings from the house in Chile and tapestries purchased on credit in Beirut. Silver trays from home were used to serve food to guests. But the beautiful surroundings were not always peaceful. Panchita and Tío Ramón argued a lot; their quarrels often lasted until both parents were exhausted.[10]

Isabel attended an English private school for girls. Her friends at school had never heard of Chile and thought she came from China.[11] The teachers at the school were very strict. Students were trained to control

The family moved again when Isabel was twelve years old, this time to Beirut, Lebanon. The post soon became dangerous.

their emotions. All the girls had to memorize the Bible. When Isabel's teacher, Miss St. John, called out a chapter and verse number, the girls were expected to recite the verse immediately. This exercise improved Isabel's English. She also learned to speak French.

The school uniforms had been designed for the cool foggy weather of England, not the heat and humidity of Beirut. The girls wore heavy, clunky-looking shoes and helmet-style hats that covered their foreheads. Their dresses were long tunics made out of coarse cloth. Buttons were considered a luxury, so the girls tied their uniforms closed with strings.

Every day the girls ate unsalted rice. Depending on the day of the week, vegetables, yogurt, or boiled liver accompanied the rice. Despite the strict discipline, ugly uniforms, and boring food, Isabel liked the school's structure.

Dangerous Times

In July 1958, the political unrest in the Middle East erupted in violence. Tío Ramón ordered Isabel and her brothers to place mattresses in front of the windows because stray bullets could shatter the glass. He forbade them to step outside their third-floor apartment. Still, the children would sneak onto the balcony to watch gun battles in the streets below. Isabel and her brothers observed many horrific acts. Once, the corpse of a man with a slit throat was left in the street for two days.[12] The battles often lasted most of the day. When night came, the fighting would stop.

The political crisis came to a head when the United States Marine Corps sent a fleet to Lebanon in July 1958 in an attempt to restore peace to the Middle East. Isabel was fifteen years old. At an indoor skating rink, she skated among young men dressed in the uniforms of US Marines. Their slang was quite different from the formal English she had heard at school. One of the Marines skated up to Isabel, kissed her on the lips, and skated off. Isabel was not sure which man it was, because with their short hair and tattoos, they all looked alike to her. She decided she would like to try kissing again. It would not be soon, however. Tío Ramón ordered Isabel to stay in the house.

Despite the warring in the streets, Isabel's school stayed open. The other schools closed, and her brothers stayed home. Isabel was thankful she could go to school and escape the boredom of the house. Eventually, though,

Crisis in the Middle East

In 1958, Beirut was wracked by internal revolts. A brutal coup had taken place in nearby Iraq, and violence broke out on the border of Lebanon and Syria. Lebanon's president, Camille Chamoun, sent an urgent request to US President Dwight D. Eisenhower asking for help in fighting the Lebanese rebels. In response, Eisenhower dispatched thousands of US Marines to Lebanon to restore the peace and preserve the government.

The streets of Beirut became a war zone in 1958. Fortunately, Isabel and her brothers were able to flee to safety in Chile.

so many parents removed their children from the school that Miss St. John was forced to close its doors. The government told diplomats to send their families home because it could not protect them from the violence.

Tío Ramón arranged for Isabel and her brothers to leave on one of the last commercial flights out of the city. Panchita stayed with him in Beirut. Isabel was on her way home to Chile without her mother. On the plane, Isabel wrote a letter to her mother. From then on, no matter where she was in the world, she would write to her mother every day. The habit played a vital role in Isabel's growth as a writer.[13]

Chapter 4

EDUCATION, WORK, AND LOVE IN CHILE

Upon their return to Santiago in 1958, Isabel and her brothers were greeted with some things old, and some things new. The old was the house on Suceia Street, as well as their same strong, disciplinarian grandfather. What had changed since they left was that neither Tata nor the house was draped in black anymore. In fact, Tata had remarried, choosing a dignified lady who cooked him wonderful meals and kept the house spotless. The fact that the house and Tata had returned, in large part, to what they were when she was a child must have been a comfort to Isabel. It was important that the children feel at home on Suceia Street since, as Isabel soon learned, they would be there for a while. Her mother and stepfather had been given a diplomatic assignment in Turkey, where they would stay for some time.

Tata the Teacher

Because of the family's travels, Isabel's education had been quite unstructured. Spanish was her primary language, and she spoke some English and French. Books had been her constant companions for her entire life, and she was well read in fine literature as well as popular fiction. At Miss St. John's school, she had memorized many Bible verses. Still, according to her grandfather, her education was far from complete.

Tata decided that Isabel could finish her schooling in a year if she attended high school and was tutored by him in history and geography. She was enrolled in La Maisonette, another exclusive school for girls. When Tata found out that Isabel had never learned mathematics, he signed her up for private classes with a math tutor.

Tata had little patience during his teaching sessions. Mistakes made him angry, but if Isabel did well, he rewarded her with a wedge of Camembert cheese from his armoire.[1] Isabel and Tata enjoyed each other's company and could sit together for hours without talking. Sometimes they read. Other times they listened with glee to horror shows on the radio. During this time, Isabel devoured science fiction books. She and her grandfather grew very close.[2]

Agriculture and Romance

In 1959, sixteen-year-old Isabel passed an exam to receive her high school diploma. Although her grades qualified her to study at the university, she decided not to go to college. At that time Chilean women did not pursue careers. Isabel expected to marry, have children, and become a housewife like most of the women she knew. Her plan seemed to be right on track when she fell in love with a handsome twenty-year-old engineering student named Miguel Frías. "He was the first boy who looked at me, and I clung to him like a crab," she would later say of Frías.[3]

Allende was confused about what to do while Frías finished his university education. Tío Ramón advised her to work for a year. Isabel took his advice and got a job as a secretary at the Food and Agriculture Organization, a specialized agency of the United Nations. The FAO aimed to help agricultural workers and to improve nutrition worldwide. Allende's job involved copying forestry statistics, and she found the work boring.[4]

Allende also worked translating English romance novels into Spanish. In most of these novels, the heroes were superior to the heroines. Allende thought the heroines in these stories seemed stupid. Sometimes she changed the heroine's dialogue to make the character sound more intelligent. She also added to the stories' endings so that the heroine became independent of the hero and did some good in the world. Allende was going beyond the role of a translator—and she was fired from the job as a result.

Feminism Meets Machismo

When Allende's parents returned from Turkey, she moved into their Spanish-style colonial home on the

Allende's first job after graduating was at the Food and Agriculture Organization, part of the New York-headquartered United Nations.

outskirts of Santiago. Every day at dawn, Allende rose, dressed, and caught the bus to the city. In the evenings after work, the buses were full, so she began stopping off at her grandfather's house to wait for a later bus. Soon she was visiting her grandfather every day for tea and conversation.

Allende has called her relationship with her grandfather "enraged intimacy" because the two had so many arguments about politics and the role of women in society.[5] Tata believed that men were superior to women in every way, and because women were helpless, men should take care of them. He believed that women should stay home and take care of the house while men pursue careers. His beliefs sprang from a worldview known as *machismo* in Spanish.

Allende rebelled against Chile's system of patriarchy. She did not intend to live her life at the whims of men. She refused to become a dependent victim, as she believed her mother had been. She demanded her grandfather's respect. Both of them were stubborn in their opinions. Despite their many disagreements, however, Isabel and her grandfather loved each other deeply.

Tata told Isabel stories about his life, too, and Isabel loved listening to him talk.[6] She was fascinated by the way he had lived. His memories brought the past to life for her. He was a constant source of inspiration. "My daily visits with Tata provided me with enough material for all the books I have written, possibly for all I will ever write," she said later.[7]

Newlywed Thrust Into the Limelight

On September 8, 1962, at the age of twenty, Isabel Allende married Miguel Frías. Because her father was absent from her life, Uncle Salvador stood in for him at the wedding. In an unusual move for her culture, she did not add her husband's last name to her own. Using only her own name was a symbol of her anger at the idea that men held the power in society.[8]

When Panchita and Tío Ramón were assigned to Switzerland, they left their beautiful colonial home in Chile to the newlyweds with six months rent paid. The young couple was gone all day: Frías at engineering school and Allende at the Food and Agriculture Organization. One day, thieves broke into the empty house and stole food and furniture. Luckily, they did not steal Memé's treasured silver mirror.

In the Department of Information at the Food and Agriculture Organization, two journalists took Allende under their wing and taught her to write articles. Journalism would turn out to be important to Allende's training as a novelist. A newswriter must grab her audience quickly and keep readers interested until the very end, a necessary skill in writing fiction as well.

Shortly after Allende started writing for the FAO's Department of Information, television stations began broadcasting in Chile. One day, the United Nations was

History of the United Nations

The name United Nations was coined by United States President Franklin D. Roosevelt. On January 1, 1942, twenty-six countries joined in the Declaration by United Nations in fighting World War II. In 1945, immediately after the war, the United Nations Charter was established, setting out the organization's policy and structure. Keeping peace among the nations of the world was the major goal of the United Nations. The organization also aimed to solve international economic, social, cultural, and humanitarian problems. Although its peacekeeping efforts have not always been successful, the United Nations—which today consists of 193 member countries—remains a forum for debate among the nations of the world.

offered fifteen minutes to explain the World Campaign Against Hunger. Ordinarily, Allende's boss would have appeared on the air, but he was ill. Allende had to fill in for him with no advance warning. She did so well that she was offered a weekly spot on television.

In her new job, Allende was responsible for all aspects of her program, from the script to the on-air delivery. For fifteen minutes a week, she appeared on television, talking about things that interested her.[9] Allende wanted to know about everything going on in the world. News, politics, and the community—all fascinated her. Her career as a television journalist was taking off.

Young Family on the Move

In 1963, Allende dreamed she would give birth to a daughter: a "slender child, with dark hair, large black eyes, and a limpid gaze." Her prediction proved to be correct. Shortly after her dream, she learned she was pregnant. On October 22, 1963, Paula was born. Later, in her book *Paula*, Allende would write to her daughter: "Those months you were inside me were a time of perfect happiness."[10]

When Allende returned to work, she felt torn between her job and her desire to be the perfect wife and mother. Sometimes she called in sick so she could spend the day with her baby. Over the course of the next year and a half, however, Allende worked regularly enough to appear on television every week. She had become somewhat of a celebrity, and people began to recognize her on the street.

As she started her family, Allende's career as a journalist blossomed. Her curiosity served her well, both in her career and in her travels.

After Allende's husband graduated from engineering school, the young couple was eager for adventure. Allende and Frías both applied for scholarships to study in Europe. Paula was almost two when the family began to travel, flying to Geneva, Switzerland. Tío Ramón met them at the airport. The family divided its time between Switzerland, where Allende's parents now lived, and Belgium, where they rented a tiny attic apartment above a barbershop. In Belgium, Frías studied engineering, and Allende took a course in television.

When classes were not in session, Allende and her husband traveled through Europe in an ancient Volkswagen, camping and carrying Paula in a backpack. When Allende became pregnant in 1966 with their second child, the family decided to return to Chile.

Political and Familial Change

Back home, Allende learned that many people were excited about a wave of political change being talked about in Chile. Her relative, Salvador Allende, was a prominent politician who, while running for president, promised many reforms for poor people. Although a large segment of the population was excited about his ideas, he lost the election to the more conservative candidate.

Although Chile's conservative religious patriarchy still held strong, the country was ripe for change. One of these changes would come from women seeking a higher profile in society. The women's movement had arrived, and Allende believed in the cause from the beginning.[11] Her rebellious nature kicked into high gear with the feminist movement. "What I was feeling was like the echo of things that were happening all over the world. Women in Europe, in the United States, were writing, were fighting, were getting organized. . . . I was one of them. I was lucky enough to be born in that generation, and not in my mother's generation," she said.[12]

A son, Nicolás, was born in 1966. Frías was working as an engineer on a construction project. The family was happy and secure. Before long, Paula and Nicolás

Allende was growing as a journalist and a feminist when the women's movement hit its stride around the world.

would be running around the garden, climbing trees, and pitching tents. Frías's parents lived a block away, on a golf course. They would provide fresh-baked rolls for the children to snack on and an inviting place to play. In the upcoming years, Allende would again juggle motherhood with her journalism career.

Chapter 5

FINDING, THEN LOSING, HER VOICE

Delia Vergara was a leading feminist in Chile in the 1960s, and also happened to be a friend of Allende's mother. Vergara knew Allende was a fairly accomplished writer whose sense of humor came shining through the pieces that she wrote. When she started the pro-feminism magazine *Paula* in 1967, Vergara asked Allende to join the team as a staff writer.

Allende's column was titled "The Impertinent Ones." She began by poking fun at the patriarchal society in Chile, writing facetiously about different types of husbands that were commonly found throughout the country. Later columns took on weightier, more serious issues such as divorce and contraception. By writing in a humorous vein, Allende was able to address head-on topics that were not usually discussed in the media in Chile at that time. Over the course of the seven years Allende worked at *Paula*, Allende also contributed an advice column and an astrology section, the latter of which was based on the adventures of her and her friends rather than any hint of Allende having inherited any of her grandmother's talent for the psychic arts.

Critics and readers were divided into two camps when it came to Allende's work at *Paula*. There were those who admired her writing and the way she tackled sensitive topics and those that thought her work was awful. Either way, Allende's time at *Paula* would contribute greatly to her development as a writer.[1]

Meeting Her Father

One day in 1969, Allende received a call from the morgue in Santiago. A man with the last name of Allende had died. The officials immediately recognized the name and called Isabel Allende to identify the body. She assumed the dead man must be one of her brothers, who had not contacted the family in months. When she arrived at the morgue, she saw that the body was that of a much older man. She said she had never seen this man before in her life. It was not her brother. She called Tío Ramón, who met her at the morgue. He told Isabel that the man was her father.[2]

All these years, Tomás Allende had been living in Santiago. She might have passed him on the street but would not have recognized him. Even as an adult, Isabel was not able to learn why her parents had split up and her father had disappeared. All she knew was that he had strange habits that her mother could not tolerate.

Allende took her usual no-nonsense view of circumstances that might have devastated another person: "I come from a family where no one looks back. We don't have the time for that."[3] Her mother's love kept her from feeling orphaned, she said, and if her father's abandonment affected her at all, it may have been in her rebellion against and distrust of men.[4]

Living a Double Life

It was through television that Allende expressed her anger against the old ways of doing things. From 1970 to 1975, she hosted two television shows in Santiago. One was an interview program. The other took a poke at Chilean society. Allende herself was living two lives. She filled the role of conservative wife and mother at home, while on television she did a series of what she called "wild things." Allende said these outrageous scenarios were not created to publicize her television program or to attract attention. It was more that she had found an outlet for her feelings of rage and rebelliousness.[5]

Her humorous television program had different names over the years. Two were *Fíjate qu* (Listen Up!) and *La media naranja* (My Better Half). Allende and actress Margara Ureta created scenes, using a candid camera, to prove their point that Chilean men often took a shallow and hypocritical view of women. For one show, Ureta walked down the street in a pair of old jeans

Back in Chile, Allende's fame quotient rose when she became the host of two popular television programs.

and a blouse. Then she changed into a miniskirt and walked down the same street. When Ureta was wearing the old jeans, the men in the area ignored her. But dressed in a miniskirt, wig, and false eyelashes, she got lots of attention. Allende showed viewers that Chilean men were much more focused on exterior details.[6]

Allende's grandfather slowly adjusted to her notoriety. Tata did not like her long dresses and antique hats. He was not pleased when she painted flowers all over her car. Even more, he disapproved of her feminist philosophy. But because Allende was a good wife, mother, and housekeeper, he forgave the things that angered him.[7]

A Nightmare of a Play

In September 1970, Salvador Allende was elected president of Chile. Allende had served as minister of health and had been a senator for many years. He had run for president several times without success. This time, he swept into office under the banner of his Popular Unity coalition.

When Salvador Allende took office, he appointed Isabel's stepfather, Ramón Huidobro, as Chile's ambassador to Argentina. Panchita and Tío Ramón moved to the capital city of Buenos Aires. At this time, many diplomats were being kidnapped, and in 1971 Allende had a dream that Tío Ramón had been kidnapped. Upset by the nightmare, she stayed home from work for two days and wrote a play, called *El Embajador* (*The Ambassador*), about the kidnapping of a diplomat. In the play, as the kidnappers and their

The Hidden Truth

The "candid-camera" format for television shows is also more accurately called the hidden-camera format. A show's writers and producers set up crazy situations and then use hidden cameras to record the reaction of unsuspecting people who witness the plotted event. These shows wanted to capture "candid," or honest, reactions, usually for comic effect. Such shows became known as "candid camera" shows because of an American television show of that name, which was broadcast, on and off, for fifty years. Allende often used this candid-camera format on her show. She became a master at using humor to prove a serious point.

hostage spend a year together in a basement, they grow to understand one another.

Allende's aunt, an actress, showed an early draft of the play to a theater company, which decided to stage it. Isabel felt embarrassed hearing her dialogue read aloud by the actors. The play clearly needed more work. As she made changes in the script, Allende learned how to make her characters more realistic.[8] The play opened in Santiago in 1972.

Advice From Pablo Neruda

By the time her play had reached the stage, Allende had achieved some fame as a journalist and television personality. She was thrilled when Pablo Neruda, the most famous poet in Chile, asked her to visit his seaside home at Isla Negra. Allende planned her interview very carefully. She worked hard to come up with just the right questions to ask the great poet. She also reviewed Neruda's work and read two biographies about his life. She wrote out her list of questions and bought a new tape recorder.

When Allende arrived at Neruda's home, she was fascinated by the strange surroundings. A maze of wood and stone held the poet's collections of seashells, bottles, dolls, books, and paintings. After lunch, she asked if he was ready to be interviewed. Neruda just laughed. She had misunderstood his invitation. He had no intention of being interviewed. Neruda went on to say that Allende was "the worst" journalist because instead of reporting straight facts, she put her own slant on every story. Not only that, but if there was nothing to report, she made things up. The famous poet told Allende that she should be a novelist instead. The imagination that made her a terrible journalist would make her a terrific storyteller.[9]

From 1973 to 1974, Allende also wrote for a children's magazine, entitled *Mampato*. When the magazine's director died, Allende filled in as director for a short time. She also published two children's stories and a collection of her humorous magazine columns.

Everything Changes

Meanwhile, ominous changes had been taking place in the Chilean government. Supporters of President Salvador Allende believed he was dedicated to helping Chile's poor slum dwellers, miners, and peasants

It was Chilean poet Pablo Neruda who suggested Allende focus her talents and imagination on writing fiction.

through a socialist form of government. One of his goals was to free Chile from the foreign corporations that owned many of its profitable natural resources, mainly its copper mines.[10] Other Chileans, including Isabel Allende's grandfather and his business associates, were horrified when Salvador Allende became president. These businessmen believed President Allende's socialist policies would destroy Chile's economy.

The military forces in Chile decided to oust Salvador Allende with a military coup, a takeover of the government by force. On September 11, 1973, Chilean military forces (the junta) led by General Augusto

Salvador Allende was escorted from his palace by armed guards during the military coup in which his government was overthrown.

Pinochet stormed La Moneda, the presidential palace. Five hours later, Salvador Allende was dead, and the military junta declared itself the new government of Chile. The military junta announced that Allende had committed suicide, though his supporters suspected he had been murdered.

That morning of September 11, Isabel Allende had set out for work as usual, only to find the streets eerily empty. She imagined she had stumbled into one of the science fiction plots she loved as a teenager.[11] It was not until the afternoon that she learned of the military coup and her Uncle Salvador's death. The coup would radically change Allende's life. "The first part of my life ended on September 11, 1973," she said.[12]

Chapter 6

ADJUSTMENTS IN VENEZUELA

Under the Pinochet regime, journalists were censored, meaning they could only print or broadcast material that was approved by the government. Anyone who was suspected of being sympathetic to Salavadore Allende's Popular Unity coalition could be fired outright. Eventually, Allende herself lost both her job as director of the children's magazine *Mampato* and her job at *Paula*. Allende believed she was fired because the military government hated feminism and thought it was as subversive as socialism.[1]

Even considering she lost her means of making a living, Allende fared better than a number of her colleagues at *Paula*. Some were forced to leave the country, safe from the threat of punishment should they print something unacceptable or be declared Popular Unity sympathizers. Still others simply disappeared. Following the coup, many people simply disappeared and were never seen or heard from again. So many people disappeared that a new verb was coined to describe the event. It was said that someone "was disappeared" when they vanished without a trace.

Underground Activist

For eighteen months, Allende took part in the underground movement in Chile. People who were considered enemies of the state had to go into hiding. Allende helped them find food and shelter, allowed them to stay in her home, and drove them to escape routes out of the country. She did not realize how dangerous her activities were until she was deeply involved in the underground. As the military government tightened its reins of power, helping its enemies became even more perilous. "I knew now that if I was caught, I would be killed or tortured," she said.[2] Later, in her book *My Invented Country*, she described fear as "a permanent metallic taste in my mouth."[3]

Finally, Allende heeded the warnings that it was too dangerous for her to remain in Chile. She learned that Venezuela was home to several thousand Chileans. In 1975, Allende, her husband, and their two children fled to Caracas, Venezuela. Allende's parents also emigrated to Venezuela, moving into the apartment above hers. Allende's in-laws and her grandfather chose to stay behind in Chile. Allende would never see her beloved Tata again.

Making a New Life

Unable to find work as a journalist, Allende took a number of jobs simply to earn a paycheck. Her

Afraid of remaining in Chile, Allende and her family fled to Caracas, Venezuela, a haven for many Chilean exiles.

journalism credentials from Chile were ignored because she had no way to prove they were true. In Venezuela, she had to start from scratch. Frías found an engineering job in the interior of the country, seeing his family only on weekends. Isabel stayed in Caracas with Paula and Nicolás. She would write at night, but she ripped up most of her work and threw it away. Exiled from her country, Allende said she felt "like a tree without roots, destined to dry up and die."[4]

In Venezuela, Allende found few opportunities in journalism. She wrote a weekly humor column for the Sunday supplement of the newspaper *El Nacional* that barely paid for the postage to submit the articles. At the age of thirty-five, Allende had lost the celebrity status she had earned in Chile. In Venezuela, she was simply a person like many others, desperately seeking work.

Allende's weekly separation from Miguel Frías took its toll on their marriage. In 1978, Allende became involved with another man and moved with him to Spain. Three months later, the affair ended. With no job and no economic resources, she returned to Caracas and her husband. They determined to make their marriage work.

Conjuring the *Spirits*

In 1979, Allende was offered a job as an administrator in a school. Colegio Marroco educated primary students in the morning and secondary students in the afternoon. Allende worked both shifts, staying from seven in the morning until seven at night. Her duties included keeping the school's accounts. At this point, she firmly

Allende began work on her first novel on January 8, the day she superstitiously begins writing all her novels.

believed that women must earn their own money to achieve independence. Without economic freedom, women would remain dependent upon men. Allende worked at the school for four and a half years.

Allende was still working at Colegio Marroco on January 8, 1981, when she began writing the letters that would become her first novel, *The House of the Spirits*. Thinking of the letters as a string of beads, she ended her family saga with the same sentence with which she had begun: "*Barrabás came to us by sea . . .*" She thought that ending the story with the same sentence was like fastening a necklace.[5]

There were so many characters and events in Allende's story that sometimes she confused time periods. When Frías read the manuscript, he sketched a blueprint of the storyline and pinned it on the walls of their dining room. Allende was then able to arrange the events so they unfolded in the right order.[6]

Allende showed the manuscript to her mother, who at first was horrified at the family secrets revealed in the story. Soon she came around, however. Panchita suggested some minor changes and helped Allende choose the title.

The women in *The House of the Spirits* demonstrate unique strength of character despite their male-dominated society. When asked if the women characters in the novel are feminists, Allende replied: "All the women in my book are feminists in their fashion; that is, they ask to be free and complete human beings, to

The Author's Process

With the writing of this first novel, Allende established a habit that has stayed with her: She always begins writing her books on the date January 8, her lucky day. This is not her only writing tradition. She writes until the first draft is finished, during which time she does not socialize. Allende burns a candle as she works as a symbol of her belief that, as the storyteller, it is her job to illumine the story and bring it to life for her readers.

She also does not like clocks, so she writes for as long as the candle burns. Then she can take time off to have dinner and socialize in the evenings. Once Allende has completed three drafts of her novel, she sends the manuscript to her mother in Chile for revisions. After her mother's changes are made, the book goes directly to the publisher.

be able to fulfill themselves, not to be dependent on men. Each one battles according to her own character and within the possibilities of the epoch in which she happens to be living."[7] Allende dedicated *The House of the Spirits* "to my mother, my grandmother, and all the other extraordinary women of this story." With this book, Allende felt she had finally done something worthwhile with her life.[8]

The Second Time Is Also Charmed

By 1984, *The House of the Spirits* was a stunning commercial success. The book had been reprinted twelve times in Spanish and had been translated into French,

Allende followed up *The House of the Spirits* with her second novel, *Of Love and Shadows*.

German, Italian, and Norwegian. Readers devoured the thrilling story of the del Valle and Trueba families.

After *The House of the Spirits* was published, Carmen Balcells had told Allende that while many people can write a good first novel, the real proof of an author's talents is a good second novel.[9] Allende was determined to prove she could do it again.

Of Love and Shadows was published in Spain in 1984. The novel describes a Latin American country in the grip of a brutal military dictatorship. Allende had written *Of Love and Shadows* in response to some grisly news from her homeland. In 1978, newspapers reported that the bodies of fifteen men were discovered in an abandoned mine shaft in Chile. The corpses were *desaparecidos* (the disappeared ones) murdered during the military coup of 1973.[10] Allende imagined the women who must have searched for their husbands, sons, and fathers, and all the while they were at the bottom of the mine shaft. She could not stop thinking about the women. For Allende, the terrible discovery symbolized all who had been abducted and murdered in Chile and throughout Latin America. She began collecting news clippings about the gruesome case, and became determined to write a story about it.[11] Despite the violence in the book, Allende considered it a story about love and about unity among people.[12]

Dismissing the Critics

Although Allende's readers loved her stories, the critics did not always agree on their literary merit. Book

In *Of Love and Shadows*, Allende was inspired by the casualties of the Pinochet regime, whose families demonstrated against the dictator.

reviewers for newspapers and magazines praised her work, but some scholars claimed it was superficial and unoriginal. They accused her of imitating another famous Latin American writer, Gabriel García Márquez, who also used magic realism in his stories.[13] Still, these criticisms had little if any impact on the millions of readers who continued to buy Allende's novels.

A case in point was what the critics had to say about *Of Love and Shadows*, which was selling well. Most of the reviews for the book were positive. One critic noted the novel was a showcase for Allende's "profound political awareness" and called her "a born storyteller."[14] Still, some critics insisted the book was too political or too

Isabel and Gabriel

Gabriel García Márquez (1927–2014) was a Nobel Prize-winning novelist with a huge, adoring readership. Many other authors also admired him. Poet Pablo Neruda, whom Isabel Allende herself greatly admired, called García Márquez's most famous work, *One Hundred Years of Solitude*, the greatest revelation in the Spanish language since Don Quixote. So why would Allende not be comfortable being compared to such a popular, well-respected author as García Márquez? The reason for her displeasure rests in Allende's feminist roots. Early in her career, people latched on to the magical realism element and presumed she was

imitating García Márquez. Rather than making her work seem like a pale, female imitation of a popular male writer, Allende would like her novels to be considered for their own merit.

sentimental. Allende responded that members of the latter group had trouble accepting her belief that love is stronger than hatred.[15]

In 1985 an English edition of *The House of the Spirits*—translated by Magda Bogin—was published in the United States. It was an immediate hit. *Of Love and Shadows*, too, was published in English (1987) and snapped up by American readers. The English translation was done by Margaret Sayers Peden, who became Allende's regular translator. Allende would continue to write in Spanish, but from that time on, her books would always be published in English as well as in Spanish.

One "critic" who loved nearly everything Allende wrote was her mother. Tío Ramón had turned seventy, and he and Panchita had decided to go back to Chile. Allende wrote letters to her mother every day from wherever she happened to be at the time. Unlike her mother and Tío Ramón, Allende was not yet ready to return to her homeland.

Chapter 7

DAYS OF SIGNIFICANT CHANGES

Publication of her novels in English opened up scores of new readers for Allende. What's more, her books were finding their way into the academic syllabi, or course study outlines, of literature courses in several colleges and universities in the United States. She found herself in demand as a guest lecturer and writing teacher, traveling to several US colleges throughout the late 1980s. She also began to receive awards for her work. While grateful to be recognized as an author and a popular writer, the concept of being honored for writing has seemed a bit odd to Allende. "I never expected that the weird craft of writing would be of any interest to the general public," she has said, "nor that a writer could become a sort of celebrity and be expected to behave like one."[1]

Full-Time Novelist

With two successful novels, Allende could finally believe in herself as an author. When she began her third novel, she was ready to pursue a full-time literary career. Allende's personal life was not going as well. In 1987, after twenty-five years of marriage, she and Miguel Frías divorced. Allende was forty-four years old. The children, Paula and Nicolás, were young adults. Allende and Frías treated each other with courtesy and respect during the divorce and would remain lifelong friends.

That year, Allende's third book, *Eva Luna*, was published in both Spain and, later, in the United States, with the English translation done by Margaret Sayers

Allende and Miguel Frías, right, shown here with French philosopher Regis Debray in 1978, divorced after twenty-five years of marriage.

Peden. In *Eva Luna*, Allende the storyteller created a storyteller as her heroine. The book opens with Eva introducing herself to the reader: "My name is Eva, which means 'life,' according to a book of names my mother consulted." Allende quickly draws the reader into Eva's fantastic and amazing tales. Many reviewers praised the book with words such as *wonderful, elegant, exotic, sumptuous,* and *magnificent.*

Allende has said that each book she writes is triggered by a different passion or emotion. About *Eva Luna*, she said, "*Eva Luna* had a wonderful, positive feeling. That was the discovery that finally I liked being a woman; for forty years I wanted to be a man; I thought that it was much better to be a man. When I was in my forties, I discovered that I had done all the things that men do and many more, that I had succeeded in my life. I was okay. And that's what the story is about; it's about storytelling and about being a woman."[2]

Off to the States for Love

After her divorce, Allende imagined that she would spend the rest of her days alone and devoted to her work.[3] But as in her stories, the unexpected happened. San Francisco lawyer William Gordon attended a lecture Allende gave in San Jose, California. Afterward, a group from the lecture went to dinner at an Italian restaurant. Gordon had read *Of Love and Shadows* and wanted to meet the author of such a deeply romantic story. Allende found herself drawn to the handsome American lawyer who spoke fluent Spanish.

After their first date in San Francisco, Gordon drove Allende to the airport. She shocked him by asking him if he were in love with her. "Poor guy, he almost drove off the road. He had to pull over, and he said, 'What are you talking about? We just met.'"[4]

Undaunted, Allende drafted what she called a contract and sent it to Gordon. It said that she would give their relationship a try in the United States, but she had two major requirements. First, he must date only her. Second, he must allow her to redecorate his house. He agreed to both, and in December 1987, Allende moved from Venezuela to San Rafael, California, to be

Allende found love again, this time with US attorney William Gordon. Their marriage brought her to the United States.

with him. They were married on July 17, 1988. Allende was now a United States resident.

Country and Career

Meanwhile, in Allende's homeland of Chile, political change was taking place. In 1988, a plebiscite, or special vote, was held in Chile. The plebiscite had been included as a measure in the 1980 constitution proposed by the military dictator Augusto Pinochet. The question in 1988 was whether or not the people wanted the candidate appointed by the junta—meaning Pinochet—to be president. If they voted no, a democratic election for president would be held the following year. Allende was determined to vote against Pinochet in the plebiscite.[5] It could lead to the end of Pinochet's reign of terror.

Allende returned to Chile for the first time in thirteen years. To her surprise, when she and Gordon arrived at the airport in Santiago, a small crowd waited to greet them. Many fans brought copies of The House of the Spirits for Allende to sign. Allende felt ecstatic to be in her homeland again. She was thrilled that the majority of Chileans voted against Pinochet in the plebiscite. A year later, Allende would go back to Chile to vote in the country's democratic general election.[6] In 1990, democracy would be restored to Chile.

Back in the United States, while Allende was teaching creative writing at the University of California at Berkeley, she received the Library Journal's Best Book Award and the Before Columbus Foundation Award. Also in 1989, The Stories of Eva Luna was published. Eva,

In 1988, Chilean citizens cast their ballots during a plebiscite. Allende returned to Chile to vote against Augusto Pinochet.

her character from *Eva Luna*, narrated this collection of stories. Allende said each story was sparked by a different event or emotion: "By something that I had read in the news. By a story someone told me that stayed with me for a long time and in a way grew inside me. And then one day, it was ready to be written."[7]

For Allende, the most meaningful story in the collection is "And Of Clay Are We Created." It is based on a horrifying event that occurred in Colombia, South America, in 1985. The volcano Nevado del Ruiz erupted, producing a mudslide that buried a village beneath it. Thirteen-year-old Omaira Sánchez became trapped in the mud and debris. Rescuers were unable to dig her out. Omaira was imprisoned there on the side of the

Power of the Plebiscite

When Chileans voted to deny Pinochet an additional eight years as president, they did so using a special vote called a plebiscite. The word is Latin for "decree of the people." During elections, people vote for candidates of their choice. In a plebiscite, voters cast a yes or no vote on a proposed political measure. In order to assure that this type of vote truly is a decree of the people, all eligible voters must be able to participate. The majority rules, meaning that whichever option, yes or no, receives the largest percentage of votes wins. Fifty-six percent of Chileans voted "no" to Pinochet remaining in power.

mountain for three days before she died. News media witnessed this terrible event.

Allende was haunted by Omaira's eyes as she looked out from the mud that trapped her. For years afterward, Allende kept a photograph of Omaira on her desk.[8] Eventually, she understood why the girl became so important to her. The story took on deeper meaning as tragic events unfolded in Allende's own life.

Tragedy Strikes

Back when *House of Shadows* was first published, Miguel Frías—whose business had declined into bankruptcy at the time—began suffering fainting spells. A physician had told Frías he had diabetes. Then, after a niece began to have similar symptoms, the entire family was tested. The doctors discovered that Frías did not have diabetes.

He and the couple's two children, Paula and Nicolás, had inherited a rare metabolic disorder known as porphyria.

The term *porphyria* is taken from the Greek word *porphyra*—meaning "purple"—because some porphyria patients excrete dark-red urine. Patients with this disorder have an abnormal buildup of porphyrins, a chemical in the body. The symptoms vary and can include sun sensitivity and abdominal pain. At this time, there is no cure for the disease.[9]

At the time the family accepted the news calmly and went on with their lives. Allende had no idea how deeply and profoundly porphyria would affect her in the future.

On December 6, 1991, while Allende was in Barcelona, Spain, for the publication of her latest novel, *The Infinite Plan*, her daughter, Paula, was rushed to the hospital in Madrid. Paula and her husband, Ernesto, lived in Spain. At the hospital, when Paula had complications due to her porphyria, she was not given the proper medication. Her brain was severely damaged. With her mother at her side, Paula slipped into a coma.[10]

The next six months were agonizing ones for Allende as she sat by her daughter's bedside in the hospital in Madrid. Allende's mother joined her during much of her vigil, as did Paula's heartbroken young husband. Gordon traveled to Spain to be with Allende when he could.

Losing Paula

Allende began to write a long letter to Paula as she lay in the coma. It begins, "Listen, Paula. I am going to tell you a story, so that when you wake up you will not feel

Allende's world was turned upside down when her beloved daughter, Paula, died from a rare metabolic disorder called porphyria.

so lost."[11] "I wrote *Paula* without knowing that it would become a book," said Allende. "It was the journal I kept as I sat in the dark corridors of the Madrid hospital, trying to ward off the specter of death."[12]

The doctors could not revive Paula from her coma. The best that could be managed was that Paula was finally able to breathe on her own. As soon as Paula could breathe without the help of a machine, Allende brought her home to the United States. There, she consulted one doctor after another, but no one was able to help her daughter.

Writing her letter to Paula helped Allende cope with the ordeal of watching and waiting as hope ebbed away. Describing her pain helped her feel less overwhelmed by sorrow.[13] Only then did Allende realize the significance of the suffering young girl whose picture she had kept on her desk. "When Paula fell into a coma . . . I remembered the face of Omaira Sánchez. My daughter was trapped in her body, as the girl had been trapped in mud. Only then did I understand why I had thought about her all those years, and finally could decipher the message in those intense black eyes: patience, courage, resignation, dignity in the face of death."[14]

One night, Paula appeared to Allende in a dream. Paula wore her nightgown and rabbit fur slippers and sat at Allende's feet in her bed. Paula told her mother she wanted to be free to die and follow the radiant path before her.[15] The dream helped Allende understand that she must stop clinging so desperately to her daughter.

As Paula lay dying, Allende felt the presence of all those spirits who had gone on before her. On December 6, 1992, exactly one year after she had become ill, Paula died surrounded by her family, More specifically, she died in her mother's arms.[16]

From Grief Comes Everlasting Treasure

Allende always began her books on the same date: January 8. But the January after Paula died, Allende was suffering such grief that it was impossible to begin another book. Then she realized the book was right there in the pages of the journal she had written at her daughter's bedside. It was *Paula*.[17]

Every day as Allende worked to make her journal into a book, tears overcame her. Her assistant told her to stop writing, because it was obviously too painful. But Allende refused, saying the writing helped her contain and control the pain.

Allende believed that experiencing her daughter's illness and death made her a stronger person. "I have a feeling now that I can face pain in a better way," she said.[18] The experience also confirmed Allende's belief that love is the highest value. "What I learned from so much suffering was that all that is left at the end is the love that you give. Not even the love that you receive, because Paula could not give me anything. She only received. But I was left with the everlasting treasure of the love that I gave her."[19]

Chapter 8

MOVING FORWARD

As she grieved for Paula, Allende took a bit of comfort from her life in California with Gordon. Especially soothing were the natural surroundings of San Rafael and the surrounding area. Her home in the United States—with its rolling hills and the California coastline, even the flora and fauna (plants and animals)—made her feel as if she was back in her homeland of Chile.[1] The state's vibrant Hispanic culture also went a long way toward making Allende feel that she had settled in the right place.5[2] In 1993, Allende decided to make things official regarding her new homeland and became a United States citizen.

Infinitely Critical

That same year, Allende published her first novel set in the United States. Based on the life of her husband, William Gordon, *The Infinite Plan* is the story of a fictional character, Gregory Reeves, and his family. Reeves is the son of a preacher who claims life is controlled by an

Hispanic Flavor of the West Coast

The state of California has its roots in Hispanic culture. Spanish sailors first explored the coast in 1542. In San Diego in 1769, Father Junípero Serra established the first of many missions that have become popular tourist attractions in Califormia. Mexican settlers traveled to California on *El Camino Real* (The King's Highway, now called Highway 101) in the 1800s.

Today, Hispanic culture thrives in California. Every year on *Cinco de Mayo* (Fifth of May), festivities commemorate Mexico's victory after the French invaded in 1862. Throughout California, Cinco de Mayo parties and parades celebrate freedom and liberty.

"infinite plan." When the preacher becomes critically ill, the family moves into the Los Angeles barrio to live with a Mexican family. Poverty and violence stalk the young Gregory. As an adult, he lives a self-destructive lifestyle and eventually concludes, "There is no infinite plan. Just the strife of living." Finally, Gregory realizes that the only quest worth following is the quest for his soul.

Many critics noted with displeasure that in *The Infinite Plan*, Allende departed from the magic realism of *The House of the Spirits*. There were other complaints, too. However, even among the critics who did not care for the book, particularly compared to *The House of the Spirits*, a few gave Allende at least faint praise for taking on such an ambitious project.[3]

The Infinite Plan may have been criticized by reviewers and scholars, but Allende's readers did not seem to care. Her fans throughout the world bought and read the book with pleasure.

Books on Film

In January 1994, Allende was present at the birth of her third grandchild. The baby, born to her son Nicolás and his wife, Celia, came into the world in the same room in which Paula had spent her final hours. Though she would always miss Paula, Allende had a rich, full life with her husband and their children and grandchildren.

Her writing career continued to bring her many rewards, not the least of which was that her works began

Academy Award winners Meryl Streep and Jeremy Irons starred in the movie adaptation of Allende's *The House of the Spirits* in 1993.

showing up on the silver screen as well as bookstore shelves. Nearly ten years after the novel *The House of the Spirits* was published in the United States, a movie version opened in US theaters. Meryl Streep and Jeremy Irons starred as Clara and Esteban Trueba, Allende's fictional grandparents. Vanessa Redgrave, Winona Ryder, and Antonio Banderas were also featured. Movie critic Janet Maslin of the *New York Times* raved about the film, saying it was filled with "understated miracles."[4]

At first, Allende was surprised at the actors chosen for the movie, because many of them were tall and blond. But once she saw the movie, she was charmed by it. Allende was impressed with the actors' ability to bring her story to life. "My grandmother was a little woman with dark eyes, small as a dwarf. She appears in the film in the person of Meryl Streep as tall, blond, and with blue eyes. And yet it felt to me, as I watched the film, that Meryl Streep was my grandmother."[5]

Allende had a continuing sense that Memé was with her. "When I say she has been with me it's true, not in the sense that she appears like a ghost, floating and moving chains around, no. But every time that I'm at a crossroads and I'm lost and confused, I think what would she do... When I'm really frightened, I ask for protection and I feel that she has protected me. She has saved me from situations I have put myself in that were pretty risky."[6]

The world premier of the movie *Of Love and Shadows* also took place in 1994. The film starred Antonio Banderas and Jennifer Connelly. Allende was glad a woman, Betty Kaplan, directed the movie. Although *Of Love and Shadows* was a thriller, Allende said that Kaplan kept the beauty and romance of the book.

Honoring Paula

The book *Paula* was published in Spanish in 1994, and in English in 1995. The book describes Allende's experiences while Paula lay in the coma, but also weaves in personal family stories to create a memoir. She relates events that happened to her, Isabel, throughout her life up until the time Paula fell into the coma and died.

Of Love and Shadows was adapted to the silver screen in 1994. The movie starred Antonio Banderas and Jennifer Connelly.

Many critics hailed the book as another great success for Allende.

Some critics pointed out that there was more in the book about Isabel than there was about Paula. They even suggested that maybe the book should have been called *Isabel*. In response, others have pointed out that Allende's vivid storytelling highlights Paula's quietness as she lies in the coma. The writing showed the contrast in personalities between mother and daughter. Allende had been prone to flights of imagination, while Paula had lived her life in a mature and simple way.[7] Either way, there is no doubt that the book honors Paula and is a lasting tribute to the love between mother and daughter.

Paula became a best seller both in Europe and in the United States. Allende was pleased by the book's reception, but she wanted to do even more to honor her daughter's memory. She decided to use money earned from sales of the book to create a charitable foundation in Paula's honor.[8]

The Isabel Allende Foundation was established on December 9, 1996, to help people in need, especially women and children. Paula had volunteered as an educator and psychologist in poor communities in Venezuela and Spain. "When in doubt," said her mother, "[Paula's] motto was: 'What is the most generous thing to do?'" Allende created the foundation to honor her daughter's "life work, her ideals, and her compassion."[9]

The foundation helps charities provide financial aid for education, health care, and other services for women

Allende channeled her grief over losing her daughter into art with the publication of the best-selling memoir, *Paula,* in 1994.

and children in need. Tom Wilson, executive director of the Canal Community Alliance in Allende's hometown of San Rafael, called Allende an "angel" for all she has done to help women and children. He believes Allende's generous financial contributions have helped save lives.[10]

Awards and Honors

During the late 1990s, Allende was the recipient of several honors that were associated with her work, although they were not directly writing awards. Her adopted home state jumped into the award-granting fray in 1996 when the city of Los Angeles named Allende Author of the Year. The city also proclaimed that January 16 of that year was to be known as Isabel Allende Day.

In 1998, Allende won two prestigious awards in the United States. The Dorothy and Lillian Gish Prize honors an outstanding contribution to beauty and to our "enjoyment and understanding of life."[11] The award brought her a silver medallion and a cash award of $200,000. Allende also won the Sara Lee Frontrunner Award, given to those who demonstrate continuous commitment to their work and who motivate others to do the same.[12]

Chapter 9

ADVENTURES IN WRITING

In 1997, after the success of *Paula*, Allende experienced writer's block. She felt as if her stories had dried up. One night she dreamed of four Indians emerging from the heart of South America. The Indians carried a large box. As they carried the box across jungles, rivers, mountains, and villages, the box absorbed every sound. The world became quiet. All sounds were swallowed up by the box. Allende awoke believing she must go to South America to search for the box. A year later, she took a trip to the Amazon jungle in Brazil. There, the vast green world filled with exotic plants and animals restored the inspiration she needed to tell her stories.[1]

Recipes and Romance

Allende is open to taking risks and seeking new challenges as an artist. *Aphrodite: A Memoir of the*

Senses, published in English in 1998, was very different from her novels and from her memoir about Paula. *Aphrodite* is a combination cookbook and memoir. Allende compares the themes of food and romance. Her mother contributed all the recipes. Allende has said that writing the lighthearted *Aphrodite* helped her come out of her period of mourning for Paula.[2] The book was considered delightful by many critics.

In 1999, Allende's sixth work of fiction, *Daughter of Fortune*, was published in both Spanish and English. This historical saga takes place in Chile and California during the California Gold Rush of 1849. Allende creates one of her typically strong heroines in Eliza Sommers. When Eliza becomes pregnant at sixteen, she defies the rules and customs of her time by running away to find her boyfriend. Trailing him from Chile to the California Gold Rush, she enters into a quest filled with danger and hardships. Along the way, she meets Tao Chi'en, a Chinese doctor who saves her life and becomes her closest friend and ally.

Time magazine reviewer R.Z. Sheppard wrote that Eliza Sommers "runs circles around everyone else" in the novel. He called *Daughter of Fortune* a "rip-roaring girls' adventure story" and said the book is part of the new feminist approach in literature in which girls from past generations act out contemporary values. Sheppard said that Allende writes from a woman's point of view with confidence and control and that she writes about romance as a fact of life.[3]

Margaret Peden, a former professor of Spanish at the University of Missouri, translated Allende's *Daughter of Fortune* (1988) into English.

Michiko Kakutani, writing for *The New York Times*, was not as complimentary. She called the book "a bodice-ripper romance."[4]

Approved by Oprah

On February 17, 2000, Oprah Winfrey chose *Daughter of Fortune* to be her thirtieth book club pick. Allende was the first Hispanic author to be chosen by Oprah.[5] In 2001, Allende appeared on *The Oprah Winfrey Show* as a guest author. The talk show host had many questions about Paula's illness. Allende answered them all in her gracious and open fashion, charming Oprah and her audience.

Daughter of Fortune was already a best seller, but after being chosen for Oprah's Book Club, sales shot even higher. Isabel Allende had become one of the most widely read living woman authors in the world. In fact, many critics consider Allende to be the first Latin American woman to enter publishing on such a grand scale. Like the heroines of her novels, Allende struck out on her own and fought hard to earn her independence.

Shades of Sepia

Allende's next novel, *Portrait in Sepia*, was published in 2001. Featuring some of the characters from *The House of the Spirits* and *Daughter of Fortune*, it is the third book in the trilogy involving the del Valle family. Its young heroine is Aurora del Valle, who is haunted by nightmares and cannot remember the first five years of her life. A photographer, she uses her own artistry as

A Quest for Adventure

Daughter of Fortune is what is known as a hero quest. In quest literature, the heroic character leaves his or her comfortable surroundings and ventures off into the unknown on a journey to reach a special goal. The journey may be an inner one of the heart and soul. It may also be an outer journey through dangerous territory. Allende often writes about heroes and heroines who face inner and outer obstacles yet overcome them, as she herself has done during her lifetime. *Daughter of Fortune* is about the quest for freedom, which Allende has called a recurrent theme in her own life.[6]

well as family photograph albums to solve the mystery of her early years. "There are so many secrets in my family that I may never have time to unveil them all," Aurora tells the reader in the opening chapter.[7] In the process, she matures as an artist and a woman. She also becomes the memory keeper for the family.

Allende herself knows what it is like to live in a secretive family, and recording memories is an ongoing theme in her books. Solving the mysteries of memory and searching for her own identity have been lifelong quests for the author.[8] Allende is quick to point out that no one's memory is 100 percent reliable: "If you and I witness the same event, we will recall it and recount it differently."[9]

Always a wanderer, Allende finds her roots in memory. She believes that memory and imagination are so closely intertwined that they cannot be separated: "If we were to remember without imagination, we would use no adjectives. It would be just nouns. But in life we remember the color, the flavor, the emotion. Not the facts."[10]

Andrew Ervin reviewed *Portrait in Sepia* in the *New York Times*, saying, "Isabel Allende makes it look easy."[11] The writing may look easy, but it is hard work. In fiction writing, an author must present characters that make the reader care about them. Allende does this by creating complex characters that are fascinating, not perfect. Allende's characters seem like real people to the reader because of their combination of strengths and weaknesses.

Adventure in the Amazon

Allende loved telling stories to her three grandchildren. When they asked her to write a story for them, she decided to grant their request and write a novel for young people. Allende says she created the story that runs through what became known as her Eagle and Jaguar trilogy of books for young adults using research and imagination.

Several reviewers noted that partway through the first book in the trilogy, *City of the Beasts*, Allende returns to the magic realism of her first novels. Aimed at ages ten and up, *City of the Beasts* was published in 2002. At its heart the book is an adventure story, but it is also about a boy growing up and getting to know himself. The fifteen-year-old hero is Alexander Cold. The story opens when Alex's mother is seriously ill. Alex is sent to live temporarily with his grandmother, Kate Cold. A journalist, Kate whisks Alex off to the Amazon, where they join an expedition to find a nine-foot-tall beast rumored to be killing people in the jungle. Their group includes an archaeologist, a doctor, two photographers, a rich businessman, and their guide. The guide's daughter, Nadia Santos, becomes Alex's companion in a flight of fantastic adventures in which they are kidnapped by a lost Indian tribe and then eventually find the ferocious beast.

Allende could draw from her own past to understand how Alex Cold felt in new and dangerous territory. As a girl whisked off to Patagonia by her grandfather, she had experienced exciting adventures in awe-inspiring surroundings.

Kingdom of the Golden Dragon, the second book in Allende's young adult trilogy, came out in English in 2004. *Dragon* also features Alex Cold, his friend Nadia, and his grandmother Kate. This time, the three journey to the Himalayas. There, they are confronted with corporate villains intent on kidnapping the peaceful society's king and stealing a golden dragon from the kingdom. Reviews of the book were mixed. Allende, like all famous writers, has learned to live with the differing views of the critics and stay true to her own voice.

In the third book in the trilogy, *Forest of the Pygmies* (2005), Allende sends Alexander Cold and his grandmother to Africa, where they go on a safari and discover a society of pygmies. In *Zorro: A Novel* (2005), pirate adventures and folk stories are interlaced with Spanish history and California history to reinvent

Allende's extensive travels have in no way diminished her ties to Chile. *My Invented Country* is a love letter to her homeland.

the legendary Zorro—elegant aristocrat by day, swashbuckling hero by night.

Memories of Two Countries

In between the books of the Eagle and Jaguar series, Allende published a memoir that was inspired by her young grandson, Alejandro. She was looking in the mirror one day, counting her wrinkles, when Alejandro slapped her on the back and informed her that she was not so old. She would live at least three more years, he assured her. His comment made her laugh, but it also made her think about where she wanted to live the rest of her life.

Although she considered herself an American, Allende missed her native Chile. She decided to write a book of her memories of her homeland. Along the way, the book also revealed more recent memories of Allende's life in the United States. *My Invented Country* was published in 2003.

The library journal *Kirkus Reviews* compared *My Invented Country* to a kaleidoscope because of the colorful mix of images of Chile.[12] *My Invented Country* is not a chronological list of memories, nor is it a dry history of the country. Allende's emotions guided her writing. One of those emotions is her feeling that Chile is better than anyplace else in the world. "The first time I visited San Francisco, and there before my eyes were those gentle golden hills, the majesty of forests, and the green mirror of the bay, my only comment was that it looked a lot like the coast of Chile."[13]

Allende appreciates the differences between her two homes, the United States and Chile, and what each country offers her.

For Allende, the history of her country is also the history of her family. In *My Invented Country*, she again tells stories about her relatives: her grandmother with psychic powers; her grandfather the patriarch; her mother and stepfather, the diplomats; and her beloved children, Paula and Nicolás.

Both Chile and the United States have been favorite settings in Allende's novels. These two countries have stirred her loyalty and affection. Finally, Allende discovered that she did not have to choose between Chile and the United States. She realized, "I can have both. And I can be totally bicultural. And I can get the best of both cultures, and use both."[14]

Chapter 10

CEMENTING HER REPUTATION

Isabel Allende and William Gordon built their dream house on a hill overlooking the San Francisco Bay. They named it *La Casa de los Espíritus*, which is Spanish for *The House of the Spirits*. Here they were surrounded by friends and family. Nicolás and his family live nearby and were frequent visitors at the villa. One of her favorite places on the estate was her garden. There she had a *casita*, or "little house," which she used as her writing space.

"I have adapted to the rhythm of this extraordinary place," Allende writes of her home in California. "I have favorite spots where I spend time leafing through books and walking and talking with friends; I like my routines, the seasons of the years, the huge oaks around my house, the scent of my cup of tea . . . the siren that warns ships of fog in the bay."[1]

The Conquistadora's Tale

Allende's next book took the author back in time and back to her roots in Chile. Published in English in 2007, *Inés of My Soul* is a fictionalized account of the real-life Inés Suarez, the only woman to become a *conquistador* (soldier) during Spain's conquest of land that would become Chile in the early sixteenth century.

Allende spent years researching the book, which is a tale of love and violence. Inés travels by herself from Spain to Peru in search of her long-lost husband. When she discovers he has died in battle, Inés decides to stay, becoming the lover of a military leader. Eventually she herself becomes a warrior, committing brutal crimes against the native Mapuche Indians of Chile. Eventually, she also comes to repect the natives and their love of the land.

Allende has compared the torture and killing of the Mapuche to what happened in Chile during the military coup of 1973. She says she felt compelled to write about this horrible time in her nation's history because she believes that people can learn from history.

"I think that by writing about these kinds of things I sort of exorcise them," she told an NPR reporter in 2006, after the book had been published in Spanish. "I come to terms with the fact that there is 'evilness' in our nature, and we have to fight against it constantly, and be aware of this evil side that we all have."[2]

Reviews of the book were generally favorable. *Publisher's Weekly* stated that "Allende crafts a swift, thrilling epic, packed with fierce battles and passionate

This is an illustration of the Mapuche people of Chile, who transform the protagonist in Allende's book *Inés of My Soul*.

Four Minutes of Fame

In 2006, Allende received a phone call asking her to participate in the opening ceremonies of the Winter Olympic Games in Turin, Italy. At first she thought they had made a mistake, since she was an author and did not consider herself anything close to an athlete. As it turns out, the Olympic Committee wanted to feature women from different walks of life to carry the Olympic flag in the opening ceremony. Only three of the eight women were professional athletes, and Olympic gold medalists at that. Among the remaining five were actresses, activists, and Allende.

"In the last 20 years I have published a few books, but I have lived in anonymity until ... I carried the Olympic flag," she said during a speech at the 2007 TED Conference in Monterey, California. "That made me a celebrity. Now people recognize me in Macy's, and my grandchildren think that I'm cool." She referred to the event as her "four minutes of fame."[3]

romance."[4] Reviewers also seemed to like the creative spin Allende put on the life of the novel's real-life heroine.

Inés of My Soul marked the last time that Allende's mother acted as the author's first and most important editor. Panchita was in her mid-eighties by the time the book was published. Both mother and daughter decided it was time for the older woman to retire from her unofficial duties of editing and proofreading Allende's manuscripts.

Honors and Letters

One can only hope that her grandfather would have been proud of Allende when she received an honorary doctorate from San Francisco State University in 2008. Tata had placed great importance on education—even for a woman. Honorary degrees are given to people who are quite accomplished in their chosen field. Allende did not earn the degree by taking classes and passing tests. Rather, she was given the academic title because of her life experiences and her success as a journalist and author.

That same year, Allende was named to the board of the Cervantes Institute. Named for *Don Quixote* author Miguel de Cervantes, the institute is a nonprofit organization that promotes the study of the Spanish language. Based in Madrid, the organization has offices in twenty countries around the world. In 2009, *The Sum of Our Days* was published in the United States. Much like her first novel, *The House of the Spirits, The Sum of Our Days* is based on a series of letters, this time between Allende in the United States and her mother, who was living in Chile. The book examines the time period after the death of her daughter, Paula. Gone is the magical realism that was part of the author's letters to her Tata, which made up the first novel. In its place is an honest discussion of Allende's private thoughts, hopes, and dreams. Allende also discusses the work that has gone into writing several of the books that came before this memoir.

Beatriz Terrazas of the *Dallas Morning News* wrote that, although a work of (mostly) nonfiction, *The Sum*

In 2014, Allende received an honorary doctorate from Harvard University. Over the years, she has earned many prestigious awards.

of Our Days was written "with the same authenticity and poetry" that could be found in Allende's fiction. She further recommended that Allende was "a survivor worth reading and emulating." *Library Journal* also recommended the work, describing it as a " high-spirited, emotionally packed book."[5]

Low to High

The year 2010 had its highs and lows for Allende. The low came first, in February, when a massive earthquake hit her beloved Chile. The epicenter was off the south-central coastline, about two-hundred miles from the Santiago. Damage throughout the country was extensive. More than five hundred people died as the result of the quake, including approximately 150 from the tsunami wave that followed. The effects of the tsunami were felt all the way to San Diego, in Allende's adopted home state.

Upon hearing about the devastation in her native land, Allende flew to Chile to participate in a telethon for disaster relief. Not only did Allende take pledges as a celebrity phone-bank operator, but she also gave a sizable donation from the Isabel Allende Foundation and one from her personal account.[6]

One high came later that year with the publication of Allende's next book, *Island Beneath the Sea*. The story concerns a Haitian slave girl named Tete, and follows her efforts to find a measure of freedom, in her spirit if not in actuality. Allende says she conducted research on the book for four years, and that it was "such a heavy book to write."[7]

As usual, reviews were mixed. The *San Francisco Chronicle* called *Island Beneath the Sea* "a page-turning drama," and praised Allende for her intricate plotting and strong, passionate female characters.[8] Others did not care for the way it was written—the *Miami Herald* said it was equal parts academic thesis paper and celebrity magazine article—or the depth of its characters.[9] Also as usual, Allende's fans did not pay much attention to the critics either way, choosing to buy the book and make up their own minds.

Another high for 2010 came in the form of Allende receiving Chile's National Prize for Literature in September. First awarded in 1942, the prize recognizes the work of outstanding Chilean writers. Other recipients include poet Pablo Neruda and Gabriela Mistral, the first Latina author to win the Nobel Prize for Literature. Two years later Allende would receive another honor, the Hans Christian Andersen Literature Award. Named for celebrated Danish writer Han Christian Andersen, the award honors artistic storytelling. Allende was the second recipient of the official award, which had begun in 2010 and is given bi-annually.

Hitting Close to Home

In 2013, *Maya's Notebook* was published in the United States. This novel represented a change for Allende, in that it was not one of her sweeping historical stories but a contemporary work about a teenager living in the United States. The story has several elements that might remind readers of Allende's own life. The title character,

Allende received a Hans Christian Andersen Literary Award in 2012.
The award honors excellence in contributions to children's literature.

Maya, grows up in a house with her grandmother and grandfather. When her grandfather dies, Maya's life takes a turn for the worse. She turns to a life of crime and drugs—Allende's three stepchildren were addicts—and when she hits rock bottom, she is saved by her grandmother. The older woman takes Maya to live on an island off the coast of Chile, where Maya writes in her notebook every day to help her figure out her life.

Also published in 2013 was *Amor (Love)*, which is a kind of greatest hits compilation. Allende introduces excerpts from her previous books that deal with love and sex. The book was published in Spanish and several other languages, but English was not one of them.

Crime and Passion

Allende followed that with the crime novel *Ripper*. The book was published at the same time in Spanish and English, in 2014. As in *Maya's Notebook*, *Ripper* features a teenage protagonist, Amanda, who lives in the United States. When not reading crime novels, she spends time playing an online mystery game with friends around the world, including her grandfather in Chile. Amanda becomes involved in the investigation of a real-life serial killer that may put her mother's life in jeopardy.

Also in 2014, Allende added two new honors to her resume. She received her second honorary doctorate, this time from Harvard University, and President Barack Obama awarded her the Presidential Medal of Freedom, which is the highest civilian honor given in the United States. The honor is given to US citizens who have made

US President Barack Obama bestowed the Medal of Freedom—her adopted country's highest civilian honor—on Allende in 2014.

an outstanding contribution to the safety or national interests of the United States, world peace, cultural or other notable public or private ventures. As someone who never went to college, and who made the United States her adopted homeland, these honors must have been very special and important to Allende.

The English version of Allende's novel *The Japanese Lover* was scheduled to be published in late 2015. Set in 1939, the book tells the story of Alma, a refugee from Poland at the start of World War II who falls in love with a Japanese American boy when she travels to safety in San Francisco. The novel follows the couple as they part and reunite over the course of their lifetimes.

Living to Write

Isabel Allende has had a long and distinguished career. She is one of the most popular writers in the world, with her books translated into thirty-five languages and more than 60 million copies sold worldwide. The Isabel Allende Foundation helps people in need in her community and around the world.

Allende's life has been filled with obstacles. Yet no matter what has happened in her life, she writes consistently. Allende has devoted her life to her passion for writing: "I write to communicate, to survive, to make the world more understandable. . . . I write because if I didn't I would die."[10]

Allende has worked hard to earn her reputation as a celebrated author. Yet she believes that her most significant achievement is not her writing but the love she shares with her family.[11] When asked to explain her greatest achievement, she replied, "Motherhood." She says the success of her books is not important in the larger scheme of things. Someday, people may not read or remember her. Her love for her children and grandchildren is the most important thing in her life. Love for family is who she is as a person.[12]

Throughout her long career, Allende has always insisted that love, and understanding among all people, are her highest values. Despite the world's problems, she has hope for the future. Isabel Allende, through her words and her life, shares that hope with readers all over the world.

Chronology

1942—Born on August 2, in Lima, Peru.

1945—Moves with her mother and siblings to her grand-parents' home in Santiago, Chile.

1952—Mother remarries and family moves to La Paz, Bolivia.

1955—Family moves to Beirut, Lebanon.

1958—Returns home to Santiago, Chile.

1959—Receives a high school diploma; meets engineering student Miguel Frías; works for the Food and Agriculture Organization of the United Nations in Santiago.

1962—Marries Miguel Frías; produces a weekly television show.

1963—Birth of daughter, Paula.

1966—Birth of son, Nicolás, in Chile.

1967—Begins career as a journalist at the magazine *Paula*.

1970—Hosts and produces two television shows.

1971—Writes a play, *The Ambassador*.

1975—Family leaves Chile and goes into exile in Caracas, Venezuela.

1981—Begins writing her first novel, *The House of the Spirits*.

1983—*The House of the Spirits* is named the best novel of the year in Chile.

1984—Second novel, *Of Love and Shadows*, is published in Spain.

1985—*The House of the Spirits* is published in the United States.

1987—Divorced from Miguel Frías; *Eva Luna* is published in Spain.

1988—Marries William Gordon on July 17 in San Francisco; she moves to San Rafael, California.

1990—Returns to Chile for the first time in fifteen years.

1991—Daughter Paula is hospitalized in Spain, suffers brain damage, and lapses into a coma.

1992—Paula dies at Allende's home in California.

1993—Allende becomes a US citizen; *The Infinite Plan* is published in the United States.

1994—*The House of the Spirits* premieres in US movie theaters.

1995—*Paula* is published in the United States.

1996—Isabel Allende Foundation is established in honor of Paula; *Of Love and Shadows* premieres in the United States.

1998—*Aphrodite: A Memoir of the Senses* is published.

1999—*Daughter of Fortune* is published.

2000—*Daughter of Fortune* is selected by Oprah's Book Club, the first Oprah pick written by a Hispanic author.

2001—*Portrait in Sepia* is published.

2002—Allende receives Excellence in International Literature and Arts Award; her first young adult novel, *City of the Beasts*, is published.

2003—*My Invented Country* is published.

2004—Allende is named to the American Academy of Arts and Letters; her second book in her young adult trilogy, *Kingdom of the Golden Dragon*, is published.

2005—*Zorro: A Novel* and the third book in her young adult trilogy, *Forest of the Pygmies*, are published.

2006—Allende joins women from around the world as an Olympic flag-bearer in Turin, Italy, representing Latin America.

2007—*Inés of My Soul* is published in the United States; she speaks at the TED conference in Monterey, California.

2008—Receives honorary doctorate from San Francisco State University; she is named a board member of the Cervantes Institute, which promotes Spanish language and literature.

2009—*The Sum of Our Days* is published in the United States.

2010— *Island Beneath the Sea* is published in the United States; she participates in a televised fundraiser to aid victims of major Chilean earthquake that struck in February; she is awarded Chile's National Prize for Literature on September 2.

2012—Receives the Hans Christian Andersen Literary Award in Denmark.

2013—*Maya's Notebook* is published in the United States. *Amor* published

2014—*Ripper* is published simultaneously in Spanish and English; she receives the US Presidential Medal of Freedom; she receives an honorary doctorate from Harvard University.

2015—*The Japanese Lover* is published in November.

Books by Isabel Allende

Dates refer to publication in the United States.

The House of the Spirits, 1985
Of Love and Shadows, 1987
Eva Luna, 1988
The Stories of Eva Luna, 1989
The Infinite Plan, 1993
Paula, 1995
Aphrodite: A Memoir of the Senses, 1998
Daughter of Fortune, 1999
Portrait in Sepia, 2001
City of the Beasts, 2002
My Invented Country, 2003
Kingdom of the Golden Dragon, 2004
Zorro: A Novel, 2005
Forest of the Pygmies, 2005
Inés of My Soul, 2007
The Sum of Our Days, 2009
Island Beneath the Sea, 2010
Maya's Notebook, 2013
Ripper, 2014
The Japanese Lover, 2015

Chapter Notes

CHAPTER 1. A SPIRITUAL UNDERTAKING

1. Isabel Allende, *Paula: A Memoir* (New York: HarperCollins, 2013), p. 244.
2. Fernando González, "Latin America's Scheherazade," *Boston Globe*, April 25, 1993, 14.
3. Verónica Cortínez, "Isabel Allende," Carlos Solé, ed., *Latin American Writers*, Supplement I (New York: Charles Scribner's Sons, 2002), p. 10.
4. Isabel Allende, *The House of the Spirits* (New York: Bantam Books, 1986), p. 122.
5. Nora Erro-Peralta and Caridad Silva, eds., *Beyond the Border: A New Age in Latin American Women's Fiction* (Gainesville: University Press of Florida, 2000), p. 1.
6. Cortínez, p. 6.
7. Hazel Rochman, "The Booklist Interview: Isabel Allende," *Booklist*, November 15, 2002, 591.
8. Allende, *Paula: A Memoir*, p. 278.
9. Erro-Peralta and Silva, p. 1.

CHAPTER 2. A BUMPY CHILDHOOD

1. Isabel Allende, *Paula: A Memoir* (New York: HarperCollins, 2013), p. 7.
2. John Rodden, ed., "The Writer as Exile, and Her Search for Home," in *Conversations with Isabel Allende* (Austin: University of Texas Press, 1999), p. 171.
3. Celia Correas Zapata, *Isabel Allende: Life and Spirits* (Houston: Arte Público Press, 2002), p. 3.
4. Allende, *Paula: A Memoir*, p. 28.
5. Rodden, p. 432.
6. Isabel Allende, *My Invented Country* (New York: HarperCollins paperback, 2008), p. 68.

7. Rodden, p. 40.

8. Zapata, p. 11.

9. Marie-Lise Gazarian Gautier, "If I Didn't Write, I Would Die," in *Interviews with Latin American Writers* (Elmwood Park, IL: Dalkey Archive Press, 1989), pp. 5–24; reprinted in Rodden, p. 125.

10. Allende, *Paula: A Memoir*, p. 36.

11. Ibid., p. 33.

12. Ibid., p. 32.

13. Ibid., p. 48.

14. Ibid., p. 44.

CHAPTER 3. STORIES ON THE ROAD

1. Isabel Allende, *Paula: A Memoir* (New York: HarperCollins, 2013), pp. 58–59.

2. Ibid.

3. Bill Moyers, "Bill Moyers Interviews Isabel Allende," June 13, 2003, PBS transcript, p. 5, http://www.pbs.org/now/transcript/transcript_allende.html (August 8, 2003).

4. Allende, *Paula: A Memoir*, pp. 59–60.

5. Ibid., pp. 61–62.

6. John Rodden, ed., "The Writer as Exile, and Her Search for Home," in *Conversations with Isabel Allende* (Austin: University of Texas Press, 1999), p. 168.

7. Ibid.

8. Ibid., p. 172.

9. Alvin P. Sanoff, "Modern Politics, Modern Fables," *U.S. News & World Report*, November 21, 1988; in Rodden, p. 103.

10. Allende, *Paula: A Memoir*, p. 63.

11. Ibid., p. 62.

12. Ibid., p. 86.

13. Rosemary G. Feal and Yvette E. Miller, eds., *Isabel Allende Today* (Pittsburgh: Latin American Literary Review Press, 2002), p. 4.

CHAPTER 4. EDUCATION, WORK, AND LOVE IN CHILE

1. Isabel Allende, *My Invented Country* (New York: HarperCollins paperback, 2008), p. 111.

2. Ibid., pp. 111, 114.

3. Helena de Bertodano, "The Incredible Life of Isabel Allende," The Telegraph, January 24, 2014, http://www.telegraph.co.uk/culture/books/authorinterviews/10589928/The-incredible-life-of-Isabel-Allende.html.

4. John Rodden, ed., "The Writer as Exile, and Her Search for Home," in *Conversations with Isabel Allende* (Austin: University of Texas Press, 1999), p. 173.

5. Ibid., p. 170.

6. Ibid., p. 171.

7. Allende, *Paula* (New York: HarperCollins, translation, 1995), p. 119.

8. Juan Andrés Piña, "The 'Uncontrollable' Rebel," *Conversaciones con la narrativa chilena* (Santiago, Chile: Editorial Los Andes, 1991; reprinted in John Rodden, ed., *Conversations With Isabel Allende* (Austin, Tex.: University of Texas Press, 1999), , p. 174.

9. Ibid., pp. 173–174.

10. Allende, *Paula: A Memoir*, pp. 116, 117.

11. Katherine Martin, ed., *Women of Courage: Inspiring Stories From the Women Who Lived Them* (Novato, CA: New World Library, 1999), p. 5.

12. Bill Moyers, "Bill Moyers Interviews Isabel Allende," June 13, 2003, PBS transcript, p. 3, http://www.pbs.org/now/transcript/transcript_allende.html (August 8, 2003).

CHAPTER 5. FINDING, THEN LOSING, HER VOICE

1. Verónica Cortínez, "Isabel Allende," in Carlos Solé, ed., *Latin American Writers,* Supplement I (New York: Charles Scribner's Sons, 2002), p. 3.

2. Ignacio Carrión, "Love and Tears," *El País Semanal,* November 28, 1993, pp. 48–59; in Rodden, pp. 301–302.

3. Ibid., p. 302.

4. Ibid.

5. Juan Andrés Piña, "The 'Uncontrollable' Rebel," *Conversaciones con la narrativa chilena* (Santiago, Chile: Editorial Los Andes, 1991); reprinted in John Rodden, ed., *Conversations With Isabel Allende* (Austin, Tex.: University of Texas Press, 1999), , p. 179.

6. Ibid., p. 178.

7. Isabel Allende, *Paula: A Memoir* (New York: HarperCollins, 2013), p. 145.

8. Piña, p. 180.

9. John Rodden, ed., "Introduction," in *Conversations With Isabel Allende* (Austin: University of Texas Press, 1999), p. 1.

10. Samuel Chavkin, *The Murder of Chile: Eyewitness Accounts of the Coup, the Terror, and the Resistance Today* (New York: Everest House Publishers, 1982), p. 1.

11. Allende, *Paula,* p. 195.

12. Isabel Allende, "Speeches and Lectures," Isabel Allende Official website, n.d., http://www.isabelallende.com/ index.html (February 11, 2004).

CHAPTER 6. ADJUSTMENTS IN VENEZUELA

1. Isabel Allende, *Paula: A Memoir* (New York: HarperCollins, 2013), p. 201.
2. Katherine Martin, ed., *Women of Courage: Inspiring Stories from the Women Who Lived Them* (Novato, CA: New World Library, 1999), p. 6.
3. Isabel Allende, *My Invented Country* (New York: HarperCollins paperback, 2008), p. 157.
4. John Rodden, ed., "The Writer as Exile, and Her Search for Home," in *Conversations with Isabel Allende* (Austin: University of Texas Press, 1999), p. 39.
5. Ibid.
6. Celia Correas Zapata, *Isabel Allende: Life and Spirits* (Houston: Arte Público Press, 2002), p. 45.
7. Marjorie Agosín, "Pirate, Conjurer, Feminist," *Imagine* 1, no. 2 (Winter 1984), p. 41.
8. Rodden, p. 189.
9. Verónica Cortínez, "Isabel Allende," Carlos Solé, ed., *Latin American Writers*, Supplement I (New York: Charles Scribner's Sons, 2002), p. 7.
10. Isabel Allende, "Writing as an Act of Hope," in William Zinsser, ed., *Paths of Resistance: The Art and Craft of the Political Novel* (Boston: Houghton Mifflin, 1989), p. 50.
11. Rodden, p. 122.
12. Ibid., p. 123.
13. Cortínez, p. 1.
14. Allende, "Writing as an Act of Hope," in Zinsser, p. 50.
15. Ibid.

CHAPTER 7. DAYS OF SIGNIFICANT CHANGES

1. Isabel Allende, "Foreword," in John Rodden, ed., "The Writer as Exile, and Her Search for Home," in *Conversations with Isabel Allende* (Austin: University of Texas Press, 1999).

2. Rodden, p. 280.

3. Isabel Allende, *Paula: A Memoir* (New York: HarperCollins, 2013), pp. 297–298.

4. Fernando González, "Latin America's Scheherazade," *Boston Globe,* April 25, 1993, 14.

5. Rosemary G. Feal and Yvette E. Miller, eds., *Isabel Allende Today* (Pittsburgh: Latin American Literary Review Press, 2002), p. 12.

6. Allende, *Paula,* p. 314.

7. Rodden, p. 280.

8. Allende, *Paula: A Memoir*, p. 309.

9. "Porphyria Overview," American Porphyria Foundation, n.d., http://www.porphyriafoundation. com/overview.html (December 11, 2003).

10. Bill Moyers, "Bill Moyers Interviews Isabel Allende," June 13, 2003, PBS transcript, p. 3, http://www.pbs. org/now/transcript/transcript_allende.html (August 8, 2003).

11. Allende, *Paula: A Memoir*, p. 3.

12. Katherine Martin, ed., *Women of Courage: Inspiring Stories from the Women Who Lived Them* (Novato, CA: New World Library, 1999), p. 8.

13. Ibid., p. 9.

14. Allende, *Paula: A Memoir*, pp. 309–310.

15. Ibid., p. 315.

16. Ibid., p. 329.

17. Martin, p. 9.

18. Ibid., p. 10.

19. Rodden, p. 307.

CHAPTER 8. MOVING FORWARD

1. Isabel Allende, *Paula: A Memoir* (New York: HarperCollins, 2013), p. 300.

2. Alden Mudge, "Writing Home: Expatriate Isabel Allende Takes a New Look at Her Native Land," *Bookpage*, June 2003, 8.

3. Marjorie Rosen and Nancy Matsumoto, "Lady of the Spirits," *People Weekly*, May 2, 1994, 107.

4. John Rodden, ed., "The Writer as Exile, and Her Search for Home," in *Conversations with Isabel Allende* (Austin: University of Texas Press, 1999), p. 294.

5. Rodden, p. 383.

6. Robert Bly, *New York Times Book Review*, May 16, 1993, 13.

7. Verónica Cortínez, "Isabel Allende," in Carlos Solé, ed., *Latin American Writers,* Supplement I (New York: Charles Scribner's Sons, 2002), p. 10.

8. Isabel Allende Foundation website, n.d., http://www.isabelallendefoundation.org/english/home.html (January 27, 2004).

9. Ibid.

10. Ibid.

11. "1998 Dorothy and Lillian Gish Prize to Be Awarded to Author Isabel Allende," *La Prensa San Diego*, September 25, 1998.

12. "The Frontrunner Awards," The Sara Lee Foundation Website, n.d., http://www.saraleefoundation.org/history/awards_frontrunner.cfm (January 29, 2004).

CHAPTER 9. ADVENTURES IN WRITING

1. Isabel Allende, "On the Amazon: Snapshots of a Green Planet," Salon, April 1, 1997, http://www.salon.com/march97/wanderlust/allende970325.html (February 15, 2004).

2. "Isabel Allende Discusses New Book on Sex and Food," CNN interactive, March 31, 1998, http://www.cnn.com/books/dialogue/9803/isabel.allende/index.html (December 12, 2003).

3. Isabel Allende, "Speeches and Lectures," Isabel Allende Official website, n.d., http://www.isabelallende.com/index.html (February 11, 2004).

4. R.Z. Sheppard, "Footnotes No Longer: As Women's History Takes Root in the Canon, More Stories About the Past Take on a Female Voice," *Time*, November 15, 1999, 108.

5. Michiko Kakutani, "Books of the Times; A Single Girl Takes On the California Frontier," *The New York Times,* November 2, 1999, 7.

6. Daisy Maryles and Dick Donahue, "Fortunate Daughter," *Publishers Weekly*, February 21, 2000, 20.

7. Isabel Allende, *Portrait in Sepia* (New York: HarperCollins, 2002), p. 3.

8. Isabel Allende, "Foreword," in John Rodden, ed., in *Conversations with Isabel Allende* (Austin: University of Texas Press, 1999).

9. Isabel Allende, *My Invented Country* (New York: HarperCollins paperback, 2008), p. 179.

10. Alden Mudge, "Writing Home: Expatriate Isabel Allende Takes a New Look at Her Native Land," *Bookpage*, June 2003, 8.

11. Andrew Ervin, "Books in Brief: Fiction & Poetry; A Woman's Reconstruction," *The New York Times,* November 4, 2001, 32.

12. "Book Review of My Invented Country," *Kirkus Reviews*, April 1, 2003, 514.

13. Allende, *My Invented Country*, pp. 9–10.

14. Bill Moyers, "Bill Moyers Interviews Isabel Allende," June 13, 2003, PBS transcript, p. 3, http://www.pbs. org/now/transcript/transcript_allende.html (August 8, 2003).

CHAPTER 10. CEMENTING HER REPUTATION

1. Isabel Allende, *My Invented Country* (New York: HarperCollins paperback, 2008), p. 188.

2. Melissa Block, "Allende Reimagines Life of Conquistador 'Ines,'" All Things Considered on NPR. Posted November 2006, http://www.npr.org/ templates/story/story.php?storyId=6442719.

3. Isabel Allende, "Tales of Passion," TED 2007. Posted January 2008, http://www.ted.com/ talks/isabel_allende_tells_tales_of_passion/ transcript?language=en.

4. Staff, "Reviews: Inés of My Soul," IsabelAllende.com, http://www.isabelallende.com/en/book/ines/reviews.

5. Staff, "Reviews: The Sum of Our Days," IsabelAllende. com, http://www.isabelallende.com/en/book/thesum/ reviews.

6. Staff, "Isabel Allende Donates $500,000 to 'Chile Helps Chile' and Adds as a Telephone [Operator]" (translated from Spanish), Emol.com. Posted March 2010, http://www.emol.com/noticias/magazine/ detalle/detallenoticias.asp?idnoticia=401944.

7. Mitzi Rapkin, "First Draft with Isabel Allende," Aspen (Colorado) Public Radio, via Public Radio Exchange (PRX). Posted April 2014, https://beta.prx.org/stories/117879?play=true.

8. Staff, "Reviews: Island Beneath The Sea," IsabelAllende.com, http://www.isabelallende.com/en/book/island/summary.

9. Staff, "Editorial Reviews: Island Beneath the Sea," Amazon.com, http://www.amazon.com/Island-Beneath-Sea-Novel-P-S/dp/0061988251.

10. John Rodden, ed., "The Writer as Exile, and Her Search for Home," in *Conversations with Isabel Allende* (Austin: University of Texas Press, 1999), p. 130.

11. Isabel Allende, "Speeches and Lectures," Isabel Allende Official website, n.d., http://www.isabelallende.com/index.html (February 11, 2004).

12. Rodden, p. 461.

Glossary

affluent—Having a lot of money and/or expensive things.

decapitated—To have one's head cut off.

dialogue—The words that are spoken during a story's performance.

dictator—One who takes absolute control of a country by being cruel and destructive.

diplomat—One who works in a foreign country as a governmental representative of his or her homeland.

emigrated—Describes having moved to a new country or region.

epilogue—The final or concluding portion of a story or book.

facetiously—Describes something said as a joke, but instead of being funny is just silly or improper.

feminism—A movement seeking the same rights for women as those for men.

grieve—To feel very sad after losing someone or something.

honorary—Given as a sign of respect or to honor one's achievements.

junta—A military group that takes control of a nation's government using force.

manuscript—Written pages that together form a book, play, or some other type of story.

memento—Something that is kept as a reminder.

memoir—A written account of a person's life and experiences.

notoriety—Being well-known for doing bad or questionable things.

ominous—Having a sense that something bad is going to happen in the near future.

subversive—A person or method that is secretive in an attempt to take control or make a change.

telepathy—A way to communicate through the mind without using any words or gestures.

tsunami—A huge ocean wave that may follow an earthquake, causing plenty of destruction.

Further Reading

BOOKS

Axelrod-Contrada, Joan. *Isabel Allende (Today's Writers and Their Works)*. New York: Benchmark Books, 2012.

Benatar, Raquel. *Isabel Allende: Recuerdos Para un Cuento/ Memories for a Story*. Houston: Piñata Books, 2004.

Dziedzic, Nancy. *Feminism (Opposing Viewpoints)*. Detroit: Greenhaven Press, 2012.

Nelson, David E. *Chile (Genocide and Persecution)*. Detroit: Greenhaven Press, 2014.

WEBSITES

Isabel Allende's Official Website

isabelallende.com/en/home

Allende's website features a blog, timeline, family album, and frequently asked questions (FAQs).

Isabel Allende Foundation

isabelallendefoundation.org

Learn more about the foundation's efforts to help women and children.

MOVIES

The House of the Spirits. Directed by Billie August, 1993.

Of Love and Shadows. Directed by Betty Kaplan, 1994.

Index